THE
FORGOTTEN
CONSERVATIVE

THE FORGOTTEN CONSERVATIVE

REDISCOVERING
GROVER CLEVELAND

JOHN M. PAFFORD

REGNERY
HISTORY

Cataloging-in-Publication data on file with the Library of Congress

ISBN 978-1-62157-037-0

Published in the United States by
Regnery History
An imprint of Regnery Publishing, Inc.
One Massachusetts Avenue NW
Washington, DC 20001
www.RegneryHistory.com

Manufactured in the United States of America

10 9 8 7 6 5 4 3 2 1

Books are available in quantity for promotional or premium use. Write to Director of Special Sales, Regnery Publishing, Inc., One Massachusetts Avenue NW, Washington, DC 20001, for information on discounts and terms, or call (202) 216-0600.

Distributed to the trade by
Perseus Distribution
250 West 57th Street
New York, NY 10107

To the memory of Grover Cleveland, a Christian statesman and stalwart defender of the Constitution.

CONTENTS

FOREWORD

WHAT KIND OF PRESIDENT would veto the provision of free seed from the federal government for drought-ravaged farmers? Was Grover Cleveland, the son of a Presbyterian minister, a cold, cruel, and heartless Scrooge? Could this be the same man who once taught at the New York Institute for the Blind and cultivated a passionate, lifelong devotion to helping the sightless?

Yes indeed, one and the same. But Cleveland was no mean-spirited skinflint. He simply knew what a minority in Congress today understands: the decisive difference between government and everything else. When Cleveland swore to uphold the Constitution, he really meant it because he had read it and believed in it. He didn't stretch or bludgeon our founding document until it confessed to powers never envisioned for the federal government at home or abroad.

Mainstream historians who evaluate the men who have served as America's president give good grades to the "activists"—those who expanded the federal government, boosted taxes and spending, and imposed new bureaucracies on future generations, even if their personal character left much to be desired.

Cleveland was of a different breed, unyielding and principled almost to a fault. He worked to limit government and protect individual liberty. He was one of the most upright and trustworthy men in public life, a virtue that propelled him from mayor of Buffalo to president of the United States in four years, with a two-year term as governor of New York in between.

Cleveland said what he meant and meant what he said. He did not lust for political office and never felt he had to cut corners, equivocate, or flip-flop in order to get elected. A man who knew where he stood, he was forthright and plainspoken. The Pulitzer Prize–winning biographer Allan Nevins said of him, "His honesty was of the undeviating type which never compromised an inch; his courage was immense, rugged, unconquerable; his independence was elemental and self-assertive.... Under storms that would have bent any man of lesser strength he ploughed straight forward, never flinching, always following the path that his conscience approved to the end."

Frequent warnings of the corrupting nature of government became Cleveland's trademark. He regarded as a "serious danger" the notion that government should dispense favors and advantages to individuals or their businesses. In vetoing the seed bill of 1887 that would have appropriated a mere ten thousand dollars to aid drought-stricken farmers in Texas, Cleveland stated that "though the people support the Government, the Government should not support the people." For relief of citizens in misfortune, he felt it was important to rely upon "the friendliness and charity of our countrymen." He was, as another of his biographers, Ryan Walters, dubbed him, "The Last Jeffersonian."

In his first term Cleveland vetoed twice as many bills as all previous twenty-one chief executives combined. Most of those bills were little more than cynical attempts by somebody to get something from somebody else by governmental coercion. He disdained pork-barrel politics as zealously as today's politicians embrace it.

Honesty was the source of Cleveland's convictions. It was dishonest, he felt, for the government to spend more than it had and send its bills to future generations. So he always worked to produce a balanced budget. It was dishonest, he believed, for government to steal from people by debasing the money. So he made sure the dollar was "as good as gold." It was dishonest, he argued, to stifle competition and consumer choice by restricting imports. So he fought to reduce tariffs. It was dishonest, he said, for government to think it could spend money better than the people who earned it. So he cut taxes whenever he could. Some people wanted the government to spend any surplus it generated, while Cleveland wanted to return it to the people. Chronic surpluses he regarded as "ruthless extortion."

Cleveland maintained the highest standards in his appointments to governmental office, appointing only people whose character and qualifications were beyond reproach. The White House during his tenure was free of scandal. He had neither an enemies list nor a friends list. One of his Supreme Court appointees was Melville Fuller, perhaps the best chief justice the country has ever had.

The welfare-statists of our day have saddled us with $16 trillion in debt, a federal tax burden many times that of Cleveland's time, and a legacy of welfare programs (including corporate handouts) that have produced little more than dependency, dysfunctional families, and distorted markets. Cleveland believed that government has nothing to give anybody except what it first takes from somebody else and that a government big enough to give us everything we want is big enough to take away everything we've got.

It is doubtful that someone of Grover Cleveland's character and principles could be elected president today—a sad commentary on the state of the Republic and its people. But there is hope. By reminding us of great men like Cleveland, books like this can reawaken in Americans a lost appreciation for what makes a republic succeed and what makes it fail.

The name "Cleveland" should first bring to mind a great American president, not a city. John Pafford does us all a great service by focusing a spotlight on a man we should revere.

Lawrence W. Reed
President
Foundation for Economic Education
Atlanta, Georgia
December 31, 2012

PREFACE

I WAS BORN AND RAISED on Cape Cod about ten miles from Gray Gables, Grover Cleveland's summer residence from 1890 until 1904. As I was growing up, I gave little thought to Cleveland. A good many years passed before my casual appreciation for his conservatism, integrity, and courage grew into a deeper respect for him as a near-great president. He did not occupy the White House in times as critical as Lincoln's, and he was not as vivid and exciting a personality as Theodore Roosevelt. He never led an army, as Washington and Jackson did, and his academic achievements were trifling compared with Woodrow Wilson's. Cleveland simply did not seem particularly interesting, and the years of his presidency did not strike me as having the drama of other periods in American history.

Yet as I learned more of Cleveland, I recognized that my view of him had been too narrow. There is much to admire in him and much to learn from his life, especially in the years of his two presidential terms. His firm defense of conservative principles and his stalwart leadership in political battle provide inspiration for readers in any generation. In contrast to the philosophy and policies which later came into fashion, Cleveland's economic views were rooted in the private sector. In each executive position he held—mayor, governor, president—he held the line against expanding government and insisted on keeping both spending and taxes low. The entitlement mentality did not yet dominate politics; those who considered it their right to be supported by the productive had not yet acquired the power they would exercise within by the middle of the next century. But Cleveland's policies were not merely a reflection of his times. They were the product of his principles. A tower of resolution, he vetoed more bills in his two terms as president than all of his predecessors combined.

Two books in particular stimulated my interest in Cleveland. The first was *A Lesson from the Past: The Silver Panic of 1893* by Lawrence W. Reed, the president of the Foundation for Economic Education and a good friend. Although limited in scope, this book praises Cleveland's leadership and prompted me to take a closer look at him. The other was *A Patriot's History of the United States: From Columbus's Great Discovery to the War on Terror* by Larry Schweikart and Michael Allen, which was published in 2004. The authors laud Cleveland as a "presidential giant," lamenting that so many historians of recent years have dropped him from the top tier of presidents.

> Perhaps because his terms were separated by the administration of the opposing party under Benjamin Harrison, or perhaps because he simply refrained from the massive types of executive intervention that so attract modern big-government-oriented scholars, Grover Cleveland has been pushed well down the list of greatness in American presidents as measured by most modern surveys (although in

older polls of historians he routinely ranked in the top ten).
Republicans have ignored him because he was a Democrat;
Democrats downplayed his administration because he
governed like a modern Republican.

Schweikart and Allen sense a change in historical opinion, however:

> Cleveland's image has enjoyed a revival in the late twentieth
> century because of new interest by conservative and liber-
> tarian scholars who see in him one of the few presidents
> whose every action seemed to be genuinely dictated by
> Constitutional principle.[1]

On March 4, 1885, in spring-like weather, Grover Cleveland was
inaugurated as the twenty-second president of the United States, the
first Democrat to assume that office since James Buchanan in 1857,
and the last until Woodrow Wilson in 1913. His rise can only be
described as meteoric. On January 1, 1882, he had become mayor of
Buffalo, New York. Exactly one year later he was sworn in as governor of New York. What kind of man was this who rose so rapidly?
What propelled him to the pinnacle of American politics? What can
we learn from the career of a man separated from us by so many
years?

ஃஇ CHAPTER 1 ஜ்ஃ

BEGINNINGS

S TEPHEN GROVER CLEVELAND WAS born on March 18, 1837, in Caldwell, New Jersey, the son of Richard F. Cleveland, a Presbyterian pastor, and Ann Neal Cleveland, the daughter of a Baltimore law book publisher. Named after a clergyman his father had admired and succeeded, he was the fifth of nine children. When he was nineteen, he started signing his name "S. Grover Cleveland"; about two years later, he dropped the initial.

Richard Cleveland had graduated from Yale with honors in 1824 and then moved on to Princeton Theological Seminary. In 1828, he was ordained, married Ann Neal, and moved to Windham, Connecticut, where he served as pastor of the First Congregational Church. Problems with his health provoked a move in 1832 to the milder climate of Portsmouth, Virginia. His health had improved by 1834, and he accepted a call from the Presbyterian Church in Caldwell. A kindly, studious man who was neither a brilliant intellectual nor a great preacher, Richard Cleveland struggled to support his large brood, but he reared them faithfully on the Bible and the Westminster Confession. Integrity and hard work were expected in this stern yet loving Calvinistic household, and Grover's Christian faith became deeply rooted. Years later, shortly before his death, he would write: "I have always felt that my training as a minister's son has been more valuable to me as a strengthening influence and as an incentive to be useful than any other incident of my life."[1]

The family moved to Fayetteville, New York, in 1841, and later to Clinton and Holland Patent, all in the central part of the state. During his boyhood years in these communities, Cleveland grew into a hearty, fun-loving young man with a strong constitution and an equally strong sense of responsibility. As a student at Fayetteville Academy and Clinton Liberal Institute, he showed himself a diligent, solid student and looked forward to attending nearby Hamilton College. In 1853, though, his father, who had been in declining health for several years, died. It now was necessary for the sixteen-year-old Grover to set aside his college plans and work to support his mother and the four siblings still at home. Although his formal schooling had ended, nineteenth-century academic standards ensured that Cleveland was well educated. For example, though not an exceptional student, he had studied Latin, working on translating Virgil's *Aeneid*. The caliber of his adult writings and speeches would be creditable for a college graduate today.

Cleveland first worked as a bookkeeper and assistant teacher in the literary department at the New York Institute for the Blind in New York City, a position suggested to him by his older brother William, who had gone to Hamilton College and had taught at the institute himself. The state-supported school taught children from poor families, and the conditions were grim. The living quarters were cold, the food was poor, and the children suffered from a lack of love and attention. Cleveland left after a year and never looked back fondly on his time at the institute. He did, however, begin a life-long friendship with another teacher, Fanny Crosby, the blind hymnist who composed such evangelical standards as "To God Be the Glory," "Blessed Assurance," and "All the Way My Savior Leads Me." Cleveland, still in his teens, impressed her with his maturity, hard work, kindness, and determination to improve himself.

Cleveland first returned to Holland Patent. Unable to find a job there, he decided to move on to Cleveland, Ohio, a city whose name seemed to call him.[2] On the way, he stopped in Buffalo to visit an uncle, Lewis Allen, a prosperous cattle breeder with a farm at Black Rock, just outside the city.

Cleveland's decision to stop in Buffalo proved providential. The city, says H. Paul Jeffers, was a perfect match for the young man:

> Bustling, uncouth, materialistic, hardworking Buffalo stood on the cusp of the rugged Western frontier and the conservative, refined East. It offered little in the way of surface graces but brimmed with people of common sense, tenacity, and stubborn character. These traits harmonized with Grover Cleveland's spirit of independence, conscientiousness, efficiency, and, above all, honesty....[3]

Situated on the shores of Lake Erie and the second-largest city in New York, Buffalo was still rough around the edges—not much in the way of museums and classical music, but plenty of bars and brothels. It was developing, though, with churches and impressive homes going up. The Erie Canal, which opened in 1825, was the key to the city's prosperity. Running from Buffalo to Albany, it connected the Great Lakes with New York City and the Atlantic Ocean. This water route flourished until later in the century, when the growing railroad network superseded it.

Lewis Allen urged his nephew to stay in Buffalo and found him employment with the law firm Rogers, Bowen & Rogers. Beginning in December 1855, Cleveland performed routine tasks like copying documents while studying in the firm's law library and learning from its attorneys in preparation for the bar examination. His diligence and intelligence impressed his employers. In 1859, he earned his license to practice law. Cleveland remained with the firm until 1862, when he was appointed to his first public office, assistant district attorney for Erie County, a post in which he served for three years. He distinguished himself with his integrity, hard work, mastery of his cases, and his ability to argue persuasively before judge and jury. This was a young man with a promising future.

Cleveland was still too young to vote in the presidential election of 1856, but he supported James Buchanan, considering John Fremont, the first Republican nominee, too flamboyant. His political sympathies were a source of tension between himself and Lewis Allen, an early and ardent Republican, for whom Cleveland retained affection and appreciation in spite of their partisan differences. The young man was influenced by the memory of his father's distaste for the radicalism of many abolitionists, and his employers and professional associates favored the Democratic Party. Most important, Cleveland's conservative beliefs and temperament were more at home in the Democratic Party of that time.

The new Republican Party opposed slavery in principle, campaigning for "Free Speech, Free Press, Free Soil, Free Men, Fremont and Victory." Although their abolitionist principles were clear, the Republicans focused on simply preventing the extension of slavery. The party's first presidential nominee, John Charles Fremont, had attracted the attention of the country as a dashing, adventurous explorer of the West, as an army officer in the war with Mexico, and as a U.S. senator from the new state of California.

The Democrats alleged that a Republican victory in the national election would cause the South to secede and engulf the country in civil war. The Democratic Party straddled the issue of slavery, keeping both anti-slavery and pro-slavery elements within the fold. The party's 1856 presidential nomination went to James Buchanan, who had served in both houses of Congress, represented the United States in Russia and in Great Britain, and had been secretary of state during the Polk administration.

Complicating the election that year was the American Party—the so-called "Know-Nothings"[4]—which took a strongly nativistic stance, opposing immigration and Roman Catholicism. The Know-Nothings favored a requirement that holders of public office must be born in the United States and included a prohibition on office-holding by Roman Catholics. The party avoided the issue of slavery in its platform and nominated former president Millard Fillmore.

Victory in the November election went to Buchanan thanks primarily to the solid South. With 45 percent of the popular vote, he carried nineteen states (fourteen of them in the South) with 174 electoral votes. Fremont was the choice of 33 percent of the voters and carried eleven states with 114 electoral votes. Although Fillmore received only the eight electoral votes of Maryland, he was one of the most successful third-party candidates in U.S. history, winning 22 percent of the popular vote. As the national conflict over slavery deepened, the American Party ceased to be relevant. Its anti-slavery members moved into the Republican Party, and those who favored slavery supported the Democratic Party in the South and then secession from the United States.

In 1860, Cleveland voted for Stephen A. Douglas, the presidential candidate of the northern Democrats. The victory of Abraham Lincoln, the first Republican president, led to the secession of eleven southern states. Although not enthusiastic about the war that began in the spring of 1861, Cleveland was firmly anti-slavery, and he supported the administration's effort to defeat the South and restore national unity.

The Enrollment Act of 1863—the Civil War draft—permitted men to avoid conscription by supplying a substitute. One of Cleveland's brothers was a clergyman making little money, and two others were in the army, so his income was needed to support his mother and two sisters. This was the very hardship that the policy of substitution was intended to alleviate, and Cleveland took advantage of the exemption from military service by hiring a substitute.

It is not indisputably clear, but it is likely that the Democrats' support of a negotiated settlement that would leave the South independent led Cleveland to vote for Lincoln's reelection in 1864. The Democratic platform called for "peace without victory."[5] It also criticized the Lincoln administration for enlisting blacks in the army. The party made a gesture for unity by nominating General George McClellan for president and Representative George Pendleton of Ohio for vice president. McClellan had broken with Lincoln over the conduct of the war (Lincoln considered him too dilatory), but he did favor winning the war, one of a minority of Democrats who supported that stance. Pendleton stood with the majority of Democrats who wanted to end the bloodshed even if that meant the loss of the South.

As the Democrats adjourned their national convention in August 1864, their prospects for victory in November appeared bright, and Lincoln feared the worst. Although the blockade of southern ports was strangling the Confederacy and the Union's control of the Mississippi had cut the South in two, it nevertheless appeared to many voters in the summer of 1864 that the war had stagnated. In Virginia, Ulysses S. Grant's army could not crush the Confederates under Robert E. Lee, and casualties were mounting rapidly. William Tecumseh Sherman's invasion of northern Georgia was being parried skillfully by Confederate General Joseph E. Johnston, who inflicted heavy losses on the invaders. But the tide eventually turned, just in time for Lincoln's electoral fortunes. On August 5, Admiral David Farragut seized the Mobile Confederates' last major port on the Gulf of Mexico, and on September 8, Sherman's army occupied Atlanta. McClellan received a mere 45 percent of the popular vote in November, carrying only New Jersey, Delaware, and Kentucky. The war would end before the middle of the following year.

Cleveland was the Democratic nominee for Erie County district attorney in 1865. He lost a close race in the Republican county and returned to his law practice, which prospered as his reputation for integrity and ability spread. In 1869, he entered into a partnership with Albert P. Laning and Oscar Folsom, the father of his future wife.

In 1870, Cleveland accepted the Democratic Party nomination for Erie County sheriff and won the general election. The position offered plenty of free time during which he continued his studies, making up for his limited formal education. During his three-year term, Cleveland had to hang two convicted murderers. He did not oppose capital punishment, but he found the duty of execution unpleasant. By the end of his term, Cleveland's reputation for honesty, ability, and strength had grown. Content with the experience gained, he declined to run for reelection, recognizing, in all likelihood, that the opportunities for growth and advancement in a second term were limited. Once again he returned to private practice.

Cleveland did not see the legal profession simply as a way to earn a living but rather as a calling. He certainly had no objection to prosperity, but his sense of justice was preeminent. He would not accept a client unless he believed him to be in the right. In time his reputation for ability, honesty, and hard work made him one of the most successful lawyers in Buffalo.

Cleveland's capacity for work was impressive. After a full day in the office, he could work through the night, take a bath, drink some coffee, and be back in the office at eight o'clock the next morning. Still, the jovial, fun-loving bachelor could play as hard as he worked, and he enjoyed the social life of Buffalo's beer halls. With one important exception, however, women seem not to have figured in his social life.

That exception was Maria Halpin, an attractive, educated widow of thirty-three who moved to Buffalo from Jersey City in 1871. She worked as a clerk and then as the manager of the cloak department at Flint and Kent, a department store. She was involved with a number of men, including Cleveland. In 1874, Maria gave birth to a son and claimed that Grover Cleveland was the father. Curiously, she named the infant Oscar Folsom Cleveland. Cleveland's law partner had a notoriously wandering eye, but he was married, as were other men with whom Maria had been involved. Considering the number of men in her life, a definitive identification of her child's father was impossible. Cleveland, a financially successful bachelor, was an attractive target. It is clear that Cleveland had an affair with Maria. The judgment of historians about his paternity of her child usually reflects their favorable or unfavorable opinion of him in general. The truth about the paternity of Maria Halpin's child probably will never be ascertained.

Perhaps to protect his partner Folsom, Cleveland agreed to provide for the child. He soon learned that Maria was drinking heavily and not caring for the baby, so he took steps to have her admitted temporarily to an asylum and the boy placed in an orphanage at Cleveland's expense. The child was eventually adopted by a prominent family in western New York and grew up to be a doctor. After her release, Maria married and settled in New Rochelle, New York. If Cleveland believed that the affair was now behind him, however, he was mistaken.

In 1875, Oscar Folsom was killed in a carriage accident. He left his wife and one daughter well provided for financially. The girl, eleven years old, had been named "Frank" after an uncle. Understandably, she later adopted the more feminine "Frances." Acting as the young girl's guardian, Cleveland took an avuncular interest in her (she called him "Uncle Cleve") until she grew up, whereupon his interest developed in another direction.

In the meantime, Cleveland's law practice continued to flourish, setting the stage for his extraordinary political career. Although he was active in the local Democratic Party, he had betrayed no ambitions beyond obtaining a judgeship. But in 1881, the corruption and ineptitude of Buffalo's municipal government sent Democratic leaders in search of a strong, honest candidate for mayor who could attract broad support. Corruption was prevalent in both parties. Recent mayors, both Republican and Democratic, had been personally honest but incompetent and weak. Some men from both parties had considered forming a third party, committed to clean, efficient government. Democrats, detecting the opportunity to capitalize on this widespread disgust, approached Grover Cleveland, a man who could attract votes across party lines. At the same time, there were important Democrats who were content with the status quo. They believed the reformers were weak and ineffective. If Cleveland were the nominee for mayor, they calculated, he would lose, and the cause of reform would be dead. This proved to be a serious miscalculation.

The Democrats nominated Cleveland, and he was elected in November with the support of reform-minded Republicans who were unhappy with their party's nominee. Cleveland's reputation for honesty, courage, and knowledge of the law made him the logical choice for all who wanted Buffalo to be a better place to work and raise their families.

Soon after he took office on January 1, 1882, an enormous sewer and water project gave Cleveland the opportunity to demonstrate not only that he was honest, but also that he had the courage and fortitude to vanquish corruption. The new mayor blocked a bid that involved kickbacks to aldermen. Pressure from the press and the public forced the aldermen to reverse themselves and accept a lower bid from an honest firm.

Cleveland's vigorous exercise of the veto eliminated taxpayer funding of projects that might have been praiseworthy but that he considered beyond the legitimate bounds of government action. He objected, for example, to giving municipal funds to the Firemen's Benevolent Association, and to the Grand Army of the Republic (a Civil War Union veterans' organization) for celebrating the Fourth of July. This type of reform activity spread through the municipal government and attracted the attention of those scouting talent for a larger stage.

The governor of New York was the Republican Alonzo B. Cornell. Chester Alan Arthur, who had succeeded to the presidency after the assassination of James Garfield, sought tighter control over his home state in preparation for his own run for the White House and pressed his secretary of the Treasury, Charles J. Folger, to challenge Cornell for the 1882 Republican gubernatorial nomination. Folger won, but he alienated Republican reformers, who resented President Arthur's ties to Senator Roscoe Conkling's political machine.

On the Democratic side, the leading candidates were Roswell P. Flowers, a wealthy former U.S. Representative and the upstate favorite, and Henry W. Slocum, a Civil War general and the choice of the New York City party. Samuel Tilden, the former governor and Democratic nominee for president in 1876, was still a force in the New York party, but declining health was limiting his involvement. His close supporter Daniel Manning was state chairman of the party. The Tilden-Manning faction became disillusioned with the choice of Flowers and Slocum and started casting about for an alternative. They particularly opposed New York City's Tammany Hall machine, headed by John Kelly. Previously led by the notorious William Magear "Boss" Tweed, the organization originated in the late eighteenth-century, taking its name from Tamanend, a Delaware Indian Chief respected for his wisdom and kindness. Tammany controlled the New York City vote through a combination of election fraud, intimidation, and charitable assistance to immigrants and working class people. Cleveland emerged as an alternative unattached to Tammany or any other faction. The Tilden-Manning forces concluded that he was an honest, capable man who could appeal to the reform wing of the Republican Party and win the election. Also backing Cleveland, although for less than noble reasons, was David B. Hill, the mayor of Elmira and former speaker of the state house of representatives. He saw himself as a future governor of New York and even president of the United States, and he determined to ride on Cleveland's coattails. Hill secured the nomination for lieutenant governor.

On September 21, the Democratic Party convened in Syracuse. After two ballots, no candidate had enough votes for nomination as governor. On the third ballot, a movement of upstate delegates indicated that the tide was moving toward Cleveland. Facing the reality that Cleveland would be the party's choice, Kelly tried to make the best of the situation and threw Tammany's support to Cleveland, whom he wrongly assumed he could control. Grover Cleveland, the still new mayor of Buffalo, thus became the Democratic nominee for governor of New York.

Cleveland campaigned little, believing himself bound by his mayoral responsibilities, but he defeated Folger handily in November, 58 percent to 37 percent, with the votes of many reform-minded Republicans. Many other Republicans, disgusted with Arthur's interference, stayed home. The Democrats also captured the state legislature for the first time since the Civil War. Now the governor of the largest state in the Union, Cleveland had stepped onto the national stage. Only a bold gambler would have predicted a short time earlier that the freshman mayor of a second-tier city would rise so high so quickly.

On the evening of election day, Cleveland returned to his office and wrote a letter to his brother William. He showed a contemplative, sentimental side and came across as a somewhat lonely, reserved man who needed to confide in someone he trusted.

> My Dear Brother:
> I have just voted. I sit here in the mayor's office alone, with the exception of an artist from *Frank Leslie's Newspaper*, who is sketching the office. If mother was here I should be writing to her, and I feel as if it were time for me to write to someone who will believe what I write.

I have been for some time in the atmosphere of certain success, so that I have been sure that I should assume the duties of the high office for which I have been named. I have tried hard, in the light of this fact, to appreciate properly the responsibilities that will rest upon me, and they are much, too much underestimated. But the thought that has troubled me is, can I well perform my duties, and in such a manner as to do some good to the people of the State? I know there is room for it, and I know that I am honest and sincere in my desire to do well; but the question is whether I *know enough* to accomplish what I desire.

The social life which seems to await me has also been a subject of much anxious thought. I have a notion that I can regulate that very much as I desire; and, if I can, I shall spend very little time in the purely ornamental part of the office. In point of fact, I will tell you, first of all the matter is a business engagement between the people of the State and myself, in which the obligation on my side is to perform the duties assigned to me with an eye single to the interest of my employers. I shall have no idea of re-election, or any higher political preferment in my head, but be very thankful and happy if I can well serve one term as the people's Governor. Do you know that if mother were alive, I should feel so much safer? I have always thought that her prayers had much to do with my success.[6]

Cleveland never displayed this side of himself to the public, reticence about personal affairs being the expectation of the people and the press and respect for privacy being the expectation of political figures. The people were entitled to know his political philosophy and his position on public policy, Cleveland believed, and he was entitled to his private life.

_⌘_ CHAPTER 2 _⌘_

GOVERNOR

C LEVELAND WAS VERY MUCH his own man, but he recognized his need for someone on his staff who was honest and loyal and who could pick his way through the political minefields of Albany. He consulted Daniel Manning, who recommended Daniel S. Lamont, a journalist who had been editor of the *Albany Argus* and later served as chief clerk of the New York Department of State and as secretary of the Democratic State Committee. Under Cleveland in Albany, Lamont was private and military secretary with the honorary rank of colonel. Later, he would be secretary of war in Cleveland's second term as president.

Grover Cleveland took the oath of office as governor of New York on January 1, 1883. At a time when long and eloquent speeches were prized, his inaugural address, delivered without notes, was fewer than five hundred words. He called for vigilance by the people and pledged honest and frugal government. Cleveland spoke and wrote with clarity and vigor, but he wanted to make his mark more by his actions than by his words. In line with his commitment to good government, he made appointments based on merit more than on party loyalty. Certainly he was proud to be a Democrat, but he was no practitioner of the "spoils system"; he was one of the strongest advocates of civil service reform.

As governor, Cleveland continued the dedication to duty that he had demonstrated since his youth. On a typical day, he rose at seven o'clock, had breakfast, often with Lamont, and walked the mile from the governor's residence to the capitol, arriving before nine. He worked through the morning and took half an hour for lunch. Leaving the office at five o'clock, he returned to his residence, where he usually had dinner alone. Then he returned to his office and worked until midnight. Sundays he relaxed more, often playing poker with friends in the afternoon. During this period of his life, Cleveland's church attendance was sporadic. As much as he could, he rejected ceremonial occasions such as formal dinners and balls.

This pace, though, was punishing, and it began to wear on him. The governor's friends noticed that his color was poor, his weight was up,[1] and he obviously needed diversion and exercise. Some time fishing and hunting in the Adirondacks restored the balance between dedication to his job and the necessity of relaxation, although the weight problem persisted. Most of his reading time was devoted to the requirements of his office, but Cleveland did enjoy history, biography, and poetry.

The minority leader of the state assembly was another New Yorker who would rise dramatically to the White House—Theodore Roosevelt. Only twenty-four, Roosevelt was similar to Cleveland in belief and character, yet the two men possessed opposite temperaments and personalities. Although Cleveland was fun-loving in private, in public he was stolid, reserved, and restrained, whereas Roosevelt was ebullient and extroverted. The mature Cleveland enjoyed hunting and fishing, but he was no match for the physically dynamic and adventurous Theodore Roosevelt (few men were). Roosevelt seemed to be constantly in motion, both intellectually and physically. He wrote extensively, vigorously, and often brilliantly on a wide range of topics, especially history and nature. Cleveland's writing, always clear and precise, was mostly limited to the responsibilities of his office. He produced two books during his retirement years: *Presidential Problems* and *Fishing and Shooting Sketches*. Roosevelt was the author of more than thirty-five books. Yet on a deeper level, they were alike in important ways. Each man based his life on Christian values. Each was a man of honor whose integrity and sense of duty were backed by moral, intellectual, and physical courage.

An informal alliance across party lines arose out of Cleveland's and Roosevelt's determination to make government more honest and responsive. It was the railroad baron Jay Gould, curiously enough, who brought them together. A bill was introduced to force Gould's Manhattan Elevated Railroad to reduce its fare from ten cents to five. Roosevelt favored the bill initially. Gould was one of the more unsavory figures of the era, a man heartily disliked by reformers in both parties who wanted to strike at his growing wealth. Also opposing Gould was John Kelly's Tammany Hall, motivated not by zeal for reform but to curry favor with voters. For a rare moment, Roosevelt and Kelly, normally inveterate enemies, were on the same side.

Cleveland had no more use for Gould than did Roosevelt and favored lowering the fare, but he vetoed the bill as an unconstitutional exercise of governmental power. The railroad had met the terms of its charter, and the federal constitution prohibited states from abrogating legal contracts. Cleveland expected to be excoriated throughout the state. To his pleasant surprise, however, newspapers and the people praised his conviction. (He later worked quietly to have the charter revised so that the fare reduction could be effected.)[2]

Roosevelt recalled this controversy in his autobiography. Noting his initial support of the fare-reduction bill, he concluded, "I believe the veto was proper, and that those who felt as I did supported the veto; for although it was entirely right that the fare should be reduced to five cents, which was soon afterward done, the method was unwise, and would have set a mischievous precedent."[3]

Roosevelt was strong-willed and sometimes impetuous, but his sense of justice prevailed, and he had the strength of character to admit when he was wrong. He and Cleveland would have their political quarrels, but they would never be personal enemies.

Cleveland's reluctance for the government to meddle in private enterprise put him at odds with Roosevelt over a bill to limit the workday of streetcar drivers and conductors to twelve hours a day. The governor thought this was a matter for negotiation between the parties, not the government, and he vetoed the bill. The veto troubled Roosevelt, who was crusading against the squalid working conditions and child labor in New York City's cigar-making industry. The exploitation of poor families was so brutal that both parties supported legislation halting the production of cigars in tenements. Cleveland signed the bill, though it was later struck down by the state's high court.

Cleveland's and Roosevelt's occasional alliance produced a civil service reform act but came to an end over efforts to reform New York City's municipal government. The legislature passed several bills, which Roosevelt favored but Cleveland vetoed. Storming into the governor's office, Roosevelt vociferously presented his case. Cleveland listened patiently then explained that although he agreed with the bills' objectives, they were poorly written. A bill dealing with tenure in office, for example, stipulated two different terms for the same office. If the bills were corrected, he would sign them, Cleveland said, but as they stood he would veto them.

Roosevelt shouted that the principle of the bills must take precedence and that they must not be vetoed. Always willing to discuss matters with those who differed with him, Cleveland would not tolerate attempts to browbeat him. He slammed his fist on his desk, and, his voice reverberating through his office, he let Roosevelt know that he was going to veto the bills. Having made the point, Cleveland proceeded to ignore Roosevelt and returned to his work. This round was Cleveland's.

Despite their differences, Cleveland and Roosevelt maintained a substantial amount of mutual respect for the rest of Cleveland's life. Roosevelt, then president, attended Cleveland's funeral in 1908 in Princeton, New Jersey, giving his predecessor generous credit for his honor and courage.

Though it is Theodore Roosevelt who is remembered for his environmental concern, Cleveland set aside land near Niagara Falls as park land, preserving one of America's most magnificent natural wonders, and he protected large stretches of the Adirondacks to keep river water clean and to maintain our natural heritage for those yet unborn.

During his short tenure in Albany, Cleveland proved willing to confront those who abused their power as the heads of great corporations, promoting legislation to provide for more openness on income sources and the use of money to influence elections. He punished fraud and perjury, but he resisted attempts to make big government the solution to every problem, recognizing the dangers to freedom and prosperity.

Cleveland led a vastly different Democratic Party from the one that emerged during the 1930s. Government, he insisted, should not undertake the direct support of people. His two terms as president made evident the vast philosophical and policy gulf between himself and Franklin Delano Roosevelt. Cleveland's Democratic Party was somewhat more conservative than the Republicans.

Once again, Cleveland had barely settled into his new office when he received a call to higher office. The Democratic Party, which had lost every presidential election since 1856, was hoping for better times as the 1884 election approached. Republican administrations had won the Civil War, but the South, whose white voters were solidly Democratic, no longer was in the wilderness. Reconstruction was over, and southern white men could vote again. Much of the sectional bitterness had passed. Many Democrats now looked with great interest at Cleveland, a new name on the national scene, a man who had won election as governor of the largest state, and who had earned a reputation for honesty and strength. Cleveland, intelligent and shrewd, understood all this. While he humbly recognized the enormous pressures and challenges of the presidency, part of him relished the opportunity to accomplish more good on this bigger stage than he could have previously. Of course, any normal human being would be flattered by the praise. Cleveland, conscious of this, always labored to keep his ego subordinate to principle.

If 1884 was to be the Democrats' year, however, Grover Cleveland was not the only Democrat interested in the opportunity. Several powerful, experienced, well-known veterans of high office also saw themselves as the next president. Battle soon would be joined.

CHAPTER 3

TO THE
WHITE HOUSE

OTHER DEMOCRATS OF STATURE threw their hats into the ring, as 1884 looked to be a good year for them and their party. The Republicans were in disarray and appeared vulnerable for the first time in decades. The Democrats had come close in 1876 with Samuel Tilden, who won the popular vote, but Rutherford Hayes had won the disputed election through the decision of an electoral commission. James Garfield kept the Republicans in control with his victory in 1880, but the party split after his assassination the following year. The new president Chester Alan Arthur could not hold the party together. In declining health (he died of Bright's disease in 1886), Arthur was unable to secure the 1884 Republican nomination, which went to James G. Blaine of Maine. A commanding figure with personal charisma, he had served as speaker of the U.S. House, as a United States senator, and as secretary of state. He had lost the presidential nomination to Hayes in 1876 and to Garfield in 1880. Blaine's electoral prospects were complicated by the distrust of the reforming element in the Republican Party. Blaine and his running mate, Senator John Logan of Illinois, were able men, but both were guilty of moral shortsightedness, seeing nothing wrong with using their positions of power to further business interests from which they profited.

Logan was one of the most successful "political" generals to come out of the Civil War. He had resigned his seat in the House of Representatives when the war broke out, organized the Thirty-first Illinois Infantry Regiment, and became its colonel. Serving in the western theater under Grant and Sherman, he rose to the rank of major general and briefly commanded the Army of the Tennessee. In 1866, he was elected to the U.S. Senate. He was credited with designating May 30 as Decoration Day (from decorating the graves of veterans with flowers), now Memorial Day. Since Blaine had not served in the armed forces, Logan was chosen to attract the votes of veterans. He too, though, was widely suspected of corruption.

Prior to receiving the nomination, Blaine sent word to the celebrated Civil War general William Tecumseh Sherman that the Republican nomination could be his if he wanted it. Sherman, entertaining guests when the message came, dashed off his famous reply, "I will not accept if nominated and will not serve if elected." This no doubt was what the ambitious Blaine wanted to hear, since Sherman's decision removed a major roadblock from his own path to the nomination.

A number of prominent reform Republicans—among them the politician and journalist Carl Schurz, the preacher Henry Ward Beecher, and the historian Charles Francis Adams Jr.—could not accept the Blaine-Logan ticket. Known as the "Mugwumps," they threw their support to Cleveland, as did the usually Republican *New York Times*, *The Nation*, and *Harper's Weekly*. Theodore Roosevelt, equally disgusted, did not break with his party, but was rather perfunctory in his activities on behalf of its choice for the White House.

Earlier that year, he had suffered the devastating loss of his wife and his mother on the same day. Now he found himself in a political no-win pickle. He would, of course, come through this bleak year and move on to greatness.

The Republicans' disarray prompted several prominent Democrats to enter the presidential race. Samuel Tilden was too ill to run, but Senator Thomas Bayard, the scion of a Delaware political dynasty who had sought the presidency in 1876 and 1880, decided to try again. Also joining Bayard in the race were Representative Samuel J. Randall of Pennsylvania, the speaker of the House from 1876 to 1881; the current speaker, John G. Carlisle of Kentucky; and former Senator Allen G. Thurman of Ohio. Thomas A. Hendricks of Indiana, Tilden's running mate in 1876, waited on the sidelines in case someone should stumble. Also at the convention with their fingers crossed were Governor George Hoadley of Ohio and former Senator Joseph McDonald of Indiana.

Kelly and the Tammany bloc of delegates did their best to turn back the rising Cleveland tide. They circulated the rumor that Cleveland would lose New York since the voters of Irish background would reject him because of his anti-Catholicism. This was a canard, for Cleveland harbored no anti-Catholic bias. They also attempted to delay the convention's vote in order to give Cleveland's opposition time to coalesce. They failed, and the curtain went up.

A total of 820 delegates attended the 1884 Democratic convention, and New York's delegation of seventy-two was the largest. The former state senator and Tammany operative Thomas Grady moved that the convention abolish New York's winner-take-all rule for apportioning its delegates. The motion was defeated 463 to 322, and Cleveland's prospects brightened. His name was put before the convention in an effective but routine nominating speech by his old friend Daniel Lockwood, who had also nominated him for governor. More dramatic was the seconding speech by the Civil War general and former member of the U.S. House Edward Stuyvesant Bragg, who stirred the delegates with his declaration that people respect Cleveland "not only for himself, for his character, for his integrity and judgment and iron will, but they love him most of all for the enemies he has made."[1]

The party at that time required a two-thirds vote for nomination. In 1884, that meant 547. When the first ballot concluded at 1:30 in the morning, no one had reached that figure, although Cleveland was solidly in first place with 392 delegates. He was followed by Bayard with 170, Thurman with 88, Randall with 78, and McDonald with 56. Hendricks, not officially a candidate, received one vote. A scattering of other candidates received 35 votes. The delegates were exhausted after finishing work on the platform, listening to all the speeches, and maneuvering for their candidates, and they voted to adjourn.

Cleveland's large lead after the first ballot instilled a sense of desperation in his opponents, who nevertheless clung to the hope that he could eventually be defeated. Kelly of Tammany Hall settled on Hendricks as the man around whom to rally. With the connivance of the sergeant-at-arms, Kelly planned to pack the gallery with people who would shout "Hendricks for president!" as he appeared on the floor just before the second ballot, prompting, he hoped, a stampede away from Cleveland to Hendricks. But Daniel Manning learned of the plot and organized a counterattack. When Hendricks appeared and the gallery exploded with cheers, most of the delegates on the floor were silent, and the wind went out of the sails of Hendricks's candidacy.

Cleveland's supporters had to endure some tense moments during the second ballot. Indiana shifted from McDonald to Hendricks, but Pennsylvania moved from Randall to Cleveland. When the voting ended, Cleveland's lead had increased, but he was still seventy-two votes short of the nomination. Sensing the inevitability of Cleveland's triumph, however, the opposition fizzled. State after state received permission from the chair to change its vote to Cleveland, who received 683 votes on the revised second ballot, well over the required two-thirds. To placate the losing side, Hendricks was then nominated for vice president with the votes of all but four delegates.

Not everyone at the 1884 convention was consumed by presidential politics. Mrs. E. A. Meriwether of St. Louis addressed the convention on the subject of women's rights. If the delegates would not express their support of votes for women, Mrs. Meriwether wryly urged them to make their position clear by adopting the following resolution:

> Resolved, that we, the Democratic men of America in Convention assembled, advise and urge the Legislature of every State in this broad Union to enact such laws as will forever put a stop to the education of the women of this land, and thereby put a stop to the clamor for equal rights, as will forever close the doors of every school, public or private, to the female children of this country; we advise and urge that it be made a penal offense, punishable by fine and imprisonment, to teach any girl or child the letters of the alphabet; and that any woman convicted of reading a newspaper or book, or entering lecture halls, whether as a listener or speaker, be severely punished by law.[2]

Mrs. Meriwether's address provoked voluble expressions of disagreement, and her resolution was not adopted. The time for women's votes was still decades away, and Cleveland himself never supported female suffrage.

It was customary at that time for candidates not to be present at nominating conventions. Cleveland was in Albany when word arrived that he had won the Democratic nomination. Following a fireworks display, he addressed a celebrating crowd of backers, charging them:

> Let us, then, enter upon the campaign now fairly opened, each one appreciating well the part he had to perform, ready, with solid front, to do battle for better government, confidently, courageously, always honorably; and with a firm reliance upon the intelligence and patriotism of the American people.[3]

Both Cleveland and Blaine knew of chinks in their own armor that the other side could exploit, but the vehemence of the attacks must have come as a surprise.

The political tradition in Cleveland's time was that presidential candidates kept themselves above the fray of the campaign. (Aaron Burr, who campaigned actively in 1800, had been the exception.) James G. Blaine bucked that tradition, making speech after speech, foreshadowing the practice that would become typical a few years in the future. Cleveland, however, left most of the campaigning to his supporters. He limited his speech-making, for the most part, to New York, New Jersey, and Connecticut, crucial states where the race was close.

The famous statement attributed to Cleveland that "public office is a public trust" actually is a summary of his statements by an enthusiastic supporter, William Hudson of the *Albany Argus*. The governor approved and adopted it. The campaign of 1884, however, would not be remembered for such high-toned pronouncements, but for a sex scandal as notorious as those of Alexander Hamilton and Bill Clinton. On July 21, ten days after Cleveland's nomination, the anti-Cleveland *Buffalo Telegraph* printed lurid accusations brought by the Reverend George H. Ball, the pastor of the Hudson Street Baptist Church and a committed Republican. Ball presented Cleveland as a debauched womanizer who had seduced Maria Halpin, promised to marry her, and then abandoned her after she became pregnant. Charles A. Dana, the editor and part-owner of *The Sun* in New York City, fanned the flames of the scandal, writing, "We do not believe that the American people will knowingly elect to the Presidency a coarse debaucher who would bring his harlots with him to Washington and hire lodgings for them convenient to the White House."[4]

The story quickly made national headlines, and alarm spread among Cleveland's supporters. His friend Charles W. Goodyear wrote to him asking what to do. The candidate's response revealed his integrity and courage: "Whatever you do, tell the truth." There was no equivocation, no squirming, no parsing of words.

Cleveland neither admitted nor denied that he was the father of Halpin's son. When supporters attributed his silence to a desire to protect the reputation of his dead friend and partner Oscar Folsom, he angrily rejected the easy tactic of laying the responsibility on a dead man. Of course, he also was protecting the feelings of Folsom's widow and her daughter, Frances, soon to be Cleveland's wife.

Another clergyman, Kinsley Twining, acknowledged that Cleveland had had an affair with Halpin. While not condoning it, he observed that it was no crass seduction of an innocent woman, but a voluntary liaison with no promise of marriage. Ball's accusation backfired, and he was forced to admit that he had overreached, making a number of accusations which he could not prove. A few years later,

Cleveland won a further measure of vindication when Ball lost a libel action against the *New York Evening Post* in connection with his accusations in the Halpin affair.

Allan Nevins, the author of the standard biography of Cleveland, takes Cleveland's side in the controversy and heaps scorn on Ball.[5] Charles Lachman, on the other hand, the author of the recent *A Secret Life: The Sex, Lies, and Scandals of President Grover Cleveland*, concludes that Cleveland did indeed father Halpin's child and repeats her claim that he raped her.[6]

The depiction of Grover Cleveland as a "coarse debauchee" proved too implausible to prevail, and the scandal soon faded. The Democratic candidate faced yet another charge—that he had been a draft-dodger in the Civil War. Cleveland's explanation of why he had hired a substitute satisfied most voters, and that matter too receded from prominence. Blaine had his own scandals. He was castigated as a corrupt politician whose word could not be trusted. Unquestionably intelligent and charming and revered by his supporters, Blaine was vulnerable to charges that he had used his powerful offices to feather his nest financially. For example, while speaker of the House of Representatives, he had made a hundred thousand dollars brokering the bonds of the Little Rock and Fort Smith railroad, which not long afterward declared bankruptcy.

An especially damaging incident was the result of Blaine's inattention rather than his actual malfeasance. On October 29, just a few days before the election, Blaine, exhausted from intense campaigning, met with a group of Protestant clergyman at the Fifth Avenue Hotel in Philadelphia, where his headquarters was located. The Reverend Dr. Samuel D. Burchard of the Murray Hill Presbyterian Church in New York City addressed Blaine on behalf of the delegation, pledging him their enthusiastic support. He concluded his remarks with the statement, "We are Republicans, and don't propose to leave our party and identify ourselves with the party whose antecedents have been Rum, Romanism, and Rebellion."[7] The meeting was open to reporters. Among those present was a stenographer sent by Arthur Pue Gorman, a senator from Maryland and the Democratic campaign manager. This failure by Blaine to distance himself from Burchard's remark would cost him dearly on election day with Catholic voters. Needless to say, the castigation of the Democrats as the party of "Rum, Romanism, and Rebellion" quickly was headline news from coast to coast. Blaine, whose mother and sister were Roman Catholics, was not personally prejudiced, but his rejection of Burchard the next day was too late to avoid the damage done to his campaign, especially in New York.

Compounding Blaine's problems as the election approached was the publicity given to a dinner organized for him by the financier Jay Gould. The dinner, held at Delmonico's in New York City, fueled the anti-Blaine blaze by connecting him with men considered more as exploiters than as constructive builders of the economy.

Public policy differences between the two parties were not as substantial as they would become in the next decade. The Republicans favored a protective tariff, but Cleveland's opposition was not as pronounced as it later was. Monetary policy was a point of contention but was not yet an explosively divisive issue. There were those who favored printing paper money unbacked by either gold or silver and others who advocated unlimited amounts of silver. Both parties, though, still stood firm against these assaults on sound money.

The United States government taxed and spent far less as a percentage of the gross domestic product than it does today. Even so, there were calls for the expansion of both taxation and spending in order to increase the power of the government over the private sector and to redistribute wealth. These ideas were not yet welcome in either of the major parties, but there were third parties with radical social and political agendas.

Third parties played an important role in a number of post–Civil War elections. In 1884, the Prohibition Party siphoned off just enough votes from the Republicans to cost them New York and therefore the presidency. Its nominee, John St. John, a Civil War colonel and a former governor of Kansas, received 25,016 of his 147,482 votes in New York, which Cleveland carried by only 1,047 votes. The left wing of American politics was represented that year by the Greenback Labor Party's Benjamin Butler, a Civil War general, former congressman, and former governor of Massachusetts. An ambitious, conniving man, he previously had been both a Republican and a Democrat. Positioned well to the left of both the Republicans and the Democrats, the Greenback Labor Party called for unbacked paper money and for an income tax. It ran candidates for president in 1876 and 1880, and in 1878 won fourteen seats in the U.S. House of Representatives. Butler received 175,096 votes, drawing little support from Democrats. After the 1884 election, the Greenback movement was subsumed into the better organized and broader based Populist Party.

Tensions increased as the day of decision drew closer. The *New York World*, owned by Joseph Pulitzer, enthusiastically endorsed Cleveland, praising his honesty. The *New York Herald* expressed the attitude of many:

> We are told that Mr. Blaine has been delinquent in office but blameless in private life, while Mr. Cleveland has been the model of official integrity, but culpable in his personal relations. We should therefore elect Mr. Cleveland to the

public office which he is so well qualified to fill, and remand Mr. Blaine to the private station which he is admirably fitted to adorn.[8]

Election day was November 4, but three days passed until it was clear that Cleveland had carried New York and therefore captured a majority of the electoral votes. He took twenty states with 219 electoral votes, while Blaine prevailed in eighteen states with 182 electoral votes. The popular vote was even closer, 4,911,017 for Cleveland and 4,848,334 for Blaine. For the first time in twenty-eight years, the American electorate had placed the mantle of the presidency on the shoulders of a Democrat.

Cleveland's rise from private citizen to mayor of Buffalo to governor of New York to president of the United States in less than three years is astonishing. Everything had to break in his favor, and it did. The office of governor of New York certainly was important, but not every New York governor became president. He was a man of ability with a sterling professional reputation, but there were other such men. Other Democratic candidates had been better known in 1884, but none of them rose above the others, and the party—especially its reform wing—wanted a new face. The Republicans nominated a powerful, popular man, but he was unacceptable to the reformers in his own party. And the Prohibition Party tipped New York to the Democrats. The political stage was set in 1884 for the rise of Grover Cleveland. As always, he was ready.

Cleveland used the four months between the election and his inauguration to wrap up his gubernatorial affairs—his lieutenant governor, David Hill, was thrilled to take the next step on a career path that he expected to take him to the presidency—and to assemble the team for his new administration. This was an extraordinarily exciting and dynamic period in American history. Industrialization, urbanization, and westward development were producing rapid change, most of it constructive, as well as cultural, ethical, economic, and foreign policy challenges to be confronted and mastered.

Since most of the approximately 126,000 federal government jobs were filled by presidential appointment (civil service reform being off in the future), the president-elect was deluged by appeals from friends and from people he had never met for positions from the cabinet on down.[9] There were hard decisions to make. For example, he turned down Wilson Bissell, his good friend and former law partner from Buffalo, for a cabinet post to avoid having too many New Yorkers and giving the impression of favoritism.[10] A temporary rift between the two men resulted, but Cleveland was determined to be president of all Americans. Once he identified the right direction, he would not be shaken, no matter the cost. He understood practical politics, including patronage. Geographical balance and bringing together different elements in the party were important, but under no circumstances would these considerations trump integrity and ability.

Politics, patronage, and the exigencies of the moment have their role in every presidency, including Grover Cleveland's. But Cleveland's presidency was built on a foundation of principle. To understand the history of his administration, we must understand that foundation. His Christianity was firm and unyielding, but not profound. His faith was subjected to assaults during the course of his life, but though battered at times as in the Maria Halpin episode, the solid foundation did not crack. He was not interested in the finer points of theology:

The Bible is good enough for me: just the old book under which I was brought up. I do not want notes, or criticism, or explanations about authorship or origin, or even cross-references. I do not need or understand them, and they confuse me.[11]

This statement does not indicate as superficial a faith as one might suppose. Cleveland was reacting to the nineteenth-century "higher critical" movement, which struck at the very idea of biblical authority.

Apart from questions about his theological sophistication, could Cleveland's Christian faith be described as orthodox? One recent biographer concludes, "A deist in the Jeffersonian sense, he believed in God, but not in all the man-crafted accretions of that belief."[12]

But the evidence suggests otherwise. He was not "deist in the Jeffersonian sense." Most assuredly, he did not regard his faith as akin to that of the self-proclaimed Unitarian Thomas Jefferson. During his bachelor years, his church attendance was spotty, primarily centered on his visits with his mother. As a family man, Cleveland returned to the church-going ways in which he was raised. Most tellingly, he gave his children a foundation in the faith, instructing them that it was the basis of a virtuous life.

Cleveland was concerned about the religious foundations of the country he led. Speaking about the United States, he said:

It would not be in existence and it could not hope to live if it were not Christian in every fiber. That is what has made it and what will save it in all its perils. Whenever we have departed from this conception of life and thought, nationality has suffered, character has declined, and difficulties have increased. While slavery remained, we could not hope

fully to work out Christian ideals, and whenever we overlook the fact that "righteousness exalteth a nation," we pay
the penalty.[13]

Cleveland was both a firm Presbyterian and a believer in Christian
fellowship and cooperation across denominational lines. Addressing
the Northern and Southern Presbyterian Assemblies in Philadelphia
on May 23, 1888, he expressed his gratitude that worship services,
Sunday school, and the Shorter Catechism had been the foundation
of his upbringing. He concluded by calling for Presbyterians to come
together again as the country had done after the Civil War.[14] In
remarks to the Evangelical Alliance in Washington, D.C., on December 9, 1887, he expressed his admiration "that your efforts are not
cramped and limited by denominational lines, and that your creden-
tials are found in a broad Christian fellowship."[15]

Cleveland rejected the religious compulsion of anyone, but he was
unabashed in affirming the importance to the nation of the Christian
faith and the desirability of winning converts:

> I welcome people from every land and of every form of
> faith, but I firmly believe that, as we have done in our
> political ideas, we shall assimilate them to our religion by
> demonstrating—as Christianity at its best estate has always
> done—its superiority and its power.[16]

Clearly Cleveland was not a "multiculturalist"; he did not see all
religions as equally valid any more than he regarded all political sys-
tems as equally valid. Of course, people living in this country are
required to obey the laws of its government. He did not call for any
such requirement in reference to religious belief, recognizing that it is

one thing to regulate how people act, something entirely different to control what they believe. Just as most Americans supported the ideas of the United States Constitution, so too he looked to a similar consensus for Christianity, a consensus arrived at through voluntary adherence.

The country that Cleveland was about to lead was moving rapidly to the front rank of world powers. The opportunities in American society attracted large numbers of immigrants seeking freedom and a better standard of living. During the 1880s and the 1890s, business and industry in the United States boomed. Many familiar brand names date from that period—Quaker Oats, Pabst Blue Ribbon beer, Coca-Cola, and Ivory soap—as do baseball cards and safety razors.[17]

Railroad networks continued to expand, linking all states and opening the entire country to manufactured goods, raw materials, fuel, and food. By 1883, Western Union had strung four hundred thousand miles of telegraph lines across the continent.[18] Alexander Graham Bell received a patent for the telephone in 1876, and one of the devices was waiting for Cleveland when he moved into the Executive Mansion. While he was away during Benjamin Harrison's term, the White House got a switchboard and operator, and its gas lighting was replaced by electricity.

The dramatic development of manufacturing, improvements in transportation and communication, and growing immigration gave a boost to urbanization. New York City surged from just over a million inhabitants in 1860 to almost 2 million in 1880 and almost 3.5 million by the end of the century. Boston grew from 177,840 in 1860, to 326,839 in 1880, and to 560,892 in 1900. Chicago's population growth was especially impressive, from just under 110,000 in 1860 to over half a million in 1880, and almost 1.7 million by 1900.[19] The progressive opening of the West over the second half of the nineteenth century brought new farm land into production. At the same time, cattle ranching expanded, more mines opened, and the timber business flourished.

As the economy was transformed, the excesses of a rapacious few made it necessary to protect the common good through prudent regulation. But how to strike a balance between protecting the vulnerable and fostering the free enterprise that would enrich the country? Cleveland believed in such a balance; he came to office with a deep commitment to fostering individual liberty and free markets.

Cleveland viewed the presidency as an executive position with important powers to be exercised for the general good. The president is the only official elected by the entire country. He is a real chief executive, Cleveland believed, taking initiative and providing leadership under the Constitution, not merely a presiding officer administering a course set by Congress. Cleveland would not be a weather vane pointing in whatever direction the wind blew.

⚜ CHAPTER 4 ⚜

THE FIRST TERM

O N MARCH 2, CLEVELAND left Albany by train for Washington. Two days later, in beautiful spring weather, he took the oath of office as president on a Bible given him by his mother. In his inaugural address, which he wrote himself and committed to memory, he pledged honest government, adherence to the Constitution, avoidance of foreign entanglements, sound money, the healing of sectional bitterness, protection of the Indians as wards of the federal government, and the ending of polygamy (then a Mormon practice) as inimical to family health and morally offensive to civilized people. All in all, it was a sound, rather routine address. His adamant support of the gold standard, however, signaled a looming conflict with the proponents of the inflationary policy of free coinage of silver.

Still a bachelor, Cleveland settled into the Executive Mansion (it would not officially be called the White House until the time of Theodore Roosevelt in 1901), with his unmarried sister, Rose, temporarily filling the first lady's position of hostess.

The size of the federal government, of course, was substantially smaller than today, its scope far more limited, and security more relaxed. The office staff of the Executive Mansion numbered just over a dozen. Several times a week, after lunch, the president received for a handshake and a few words all who wished to meet him, a homely practice that continued into the period between the world wars, when the dangers of a changing world necessitated more stringent security measures.

The men he selected for his cabinet were respected for their integrity, ability, and professional achievement. It reflected well on Cleveland as an executive that he selected strong men and entrusted them with running their departments within the bounds of policies he set. He encouraged free debate in cabinet meetings, but he then made the decisions as to the course of the administration and insisted that they all then unite.

Cleveland chose Senator Thomas Bayard of Delaware, his leading opponent at the 1884 Democratic convention, to be his secretary of state. Daniel Manning, an advocate of the gold standard, was the new secretary of the Treasury. Although his health was failing (he died of Bright's disease in 1887), he accepted the position after Cleveland earnestly requested that he do so.

William C. Endicott of Massachusetts was Cleveland's choice to be secretary of war. He attended Harvard College and Harvard Law School and had served on the Massachusetts Supreme Judicial Court, though he had lost races for governor and the U.S. House of Representatives.

Augustus Garland of Arkansas became the next attorney general. He had opposed secession but stayed with his state after it left the union and served in both the Confederate House of Representatives and Senate. After the war he represented Arkansas in the U.S. Senate. The new secretary of the navy was William C. Whitney of New York, a prominent attorney, clearly identified with the reform wing of the party, a vigorous opponent of Tweed and the Tammany organization.

Allan Nevins considered Bayard, Manning, and Whitney "the backbone of the Cabinet, its ablest men, and from the beginning to the end [Cleveland's] most trusted advisors."[1]

Cleveland named William F. Vilas of Wisconsin, a graduate of the University of Wisconsin who later studied law at the University of Albany, as his postmaster general. During the Civil War, Vilas had served as a lieutenant colonel, then returned to the University of Wisconsin as a law professor. A conservative gold-standard Democrat, he was the chairman of the 1884 national convention.

A second former Confederate in the cabinet was the secretary of the interior, Lucius Q. C. Lamar of Mississippi, who had been both an army officer and a diplomat during the war. Rising to the rank of colonel in the Confederate army, he had served on the staff of his cousin, General James Longstreet. Later, he represented the Confederacy as minister to Russia. After the war, he taught law at the University of Mississippi and later was elected to the U.S. House of Representatives, where he had served prior to the secession of Mississippi. When Cleveland named him to the cabinet, he was a U.S. senator.

Of particular importance in the new administration was the loyal and capable Daniel Lamont, who moved with Cleveland from Albany to Washington, continuing as his confidential secretary. He was trustworthy, reliable in his routine duties such as making copies of the president's correspondence, and a good sounding board who could give practical advice. Always, though, Cleveland was a strong chief executive who made his own decisions.

The new president faced the challenge of a divided Congress. Although the Republican Party dominated national politics from the Civil War until Franklin Roosevelt's election in 1932, the Democrats won control of the House of Representatives in every election but two from 1874 to 1894. The 1884 election increased the Republican majority in the Senate—41 to 34, with one vacancy—and decreased the Democratic majority in the House by eighteen seats. Without the luxury of a cooperative Congress, Cleveland soon established his reputation for standing on principle. He exercised his veto power 414 times—more than twice the total of all his predecessors combined.

Cleveland's dedication to civil service reform was evident from the beginning of his first term, and on this issue his relations with Congress were not acrimonious. He supported the Pendleton Civil Service Reform Act, which the Republicans had passed in 1883, removing about 10 percent of the federal government's civilian jobs from the spoils system by making them open to those who qualified through examination. Cleveland furthered the reform cause by retaining capable Republican incumbents who were not protected by the Pendleton Act, much to the dismay of office-hungry Democrats who had been in the wilderness for almost a generation. Positions that were important for making and implementing policy, of course, went to those who not only were honest and competent, but also supported the direction in which the president wanted to move the country.

It was the issue of military pensions that provoked Cleveland's first battles with Congress and presented him with a conflict between his principles of limited government and integrity on the one hand and practical political realities on the other. In 1862, Congress had awarded pensions to Union army and navy personnel who had suffered war-related injuries. Their widows, orphans, and dependent parents also were to receive assistance. When Cleveland took office, the number of persons receiving these benefits had soared by about 500 percent—an astonishing figure, since one would have expected it to decrease with the passage of the years.[2] The enormously influential Grand Army of the Republic, boasting four hundred thousand members, supported a generous pension policy. It was politically perilous for a Democrat who had not served in the armed forces to make an enemy of the GAR. Cleveland met the problem in his typical manner, not dodging or attempting to obfuscate. He deflected much of the criticism of his not having been in uniform during the war by explaining the circumstances. Enforcing his policies of limited government and integrity, however, proved more difficult. Cleveland actually signed many more bills providing pension benefits than he vetoed. But his determined opposition to patently false claims aroused the ire of those who thought such demands on the national Treasury should be met without question. Nevertheless, Cleveland won substantial support for his courage in halting scams. Before his first term was over, he had made the case for integrity and common sense in pension spending.

Racial issues were especially difficult for a post-Reconstruction northern Democrat. The southern states were again controlled by whites who had been disenfranchised for a number of years after the Civil War. During the years of Reconstruction under the Johnson and Grant administrations, the former Confederate states had been run by northern whites who had moved south, the minority of southern whites who had remained loyal to the United States, and former slaves. With the end of Reconstruction in 1877, the white population again could vote and did so overwhelmingly for the Democrats. Blacks, who were predominantly Republican, suffered increasing restrictions on their civil liberties.

Cleveland was a moderate reformer on racial matters, supporting constitutional rights for non-whites, although he did not advocate the integration of schools. In later years he recalled that "whatever I did was in favor of maintaining separate colored schools instead of having them mixed."[3] The former slaves, he believed, were behind other Americans in their development, but he wanted to see them rise. At the same time, Cleveland knew that without the votes of the southern states, the Democratic Party could not win national elections—the presidency and the Congress would be Republican. He labored, therefore, to support the principle of black advancement without dooming his party to the political wilderness, as his relations with Frederick Douglass demonstrate.

Douglass was born a slave, probably in 1818, and managed to educate himself with the aid of his master's wife. In 1838, he fled to Massachusetts, where he attracted the support of abolitionists, and published an influential autobiography in 1845. During the Civil War, he helped recruit black soldiers for the United States and met several times with President Lincoln. Since 1881, he had served as recorder of deeds for the District of Columbia, but Cleveland came under pressure from his party to replace the black Republican Douglass. Cleveland did not replace him until later in 1886. In the meantime,

Douglass met several times with the president, with whom he was impressed in spite of their partisan differences.

> I found him a robust, manly man, one having the courage
> to act upon his convictions, and to bear with equanimity
> the reproaches of those who differed from him.... He never
> failed while I held office under him, to invite myself and
> wife to his grand receptions, and we never failed to attend
> them. Surrounded by distinguished men and women from
> all parts of the country and by diplomatic representatives
> from all parts of the world, and under the gaze of the late
> slaveholders, there was nothing in the bearing of Mr. and
> Mrs. Cleveland toward Mrs. Douglass and myself less
> cordial and courteous than that extended to the other ladies
> and gentlemen present. This manly defiance, by a Demo-
> cratic President, of a malignant and time-honored preju-
> dice, won my respect for the courage of Mr. Cleveland. We
> were in politics separated from each other by a space ocean
> wide. I had done all that I could to defeat his election and
> to elect Mr. James G. Blaine, but this made no apparent
> difference with Mr. Cleveland. He found me in office when
> he came into the Presidency, and he was too noble to refuse
> me the recognition and hospitalities that my official posi-
> tion gave me the right to claim. Though this conduct drew
> upon him fierce and bitter reproaches from members of his
> own party in the South, he never faltered or flinched, and
> continued to invite Mrs. Douglass and myself to his recep-
> tions during all the time that I was in office under his
> administration, and often wrote the invitations with his
> own hand.[4]

Cleveland's accomplishments in the field of racial progress, however, were limited to the kind of sincere but small steps that Douglass describes.

The American Indians of the West had been pacified, for the most part, by the time Cleveland became president. His policy in the short term was to protect their lands from rapacious outsiders and in the long run to promote their assimilation into the mainstream of American national life. For example, he supported English as a medium of instruction in Indian schools in order to further this integration.

A few days before he left office, President Arthur had issued an order placing a large portion of the Winnebago and Crow Creek lands on the Missouri River in the Dakota Territory in the public domain. On May 1, 1885, settlers could move in, and a good number had in fact already done so prior to that date. The Indians, understandably, were incensed and restive. After an investigation ordered by Cleveland, Secretary of the Interior Lucius Q. C. Lamar reported that rapacious whites had swindled many of the Indians. Attorney General Garland rendered an opinion that Arthur's order was illegal, so Cleveland rescinded it. Ranchers, land speculators, settlers, and anyone who had suffered from Indian raids protested, but Cleveland was firm.

Indian troubles also percolated in the southern plains, where the Cheyenne and Arapahoe reservations in what is now Oklahoma had been subjected to depredations by cattlemen who took advantage of Indian ignorance of legal procedures to gain control of part of these reservations. Cleveland sent the Civil War hero Philip Sheridan, the senior general in the army, to investigate. In his instructions to Sheridan, Cleveland was clear that the Indians were to be protected from wrongs inflicted on them by whites, though he did not assume that Indians could do no wrong:

> In view of the possible disturbance that may occur among the Indians now in the Indian Territory, and the contemplated concentration of troops in that locality, I deem it desirable that you proceed at once to the location where trouble is to be apprehended, and advise with and direct those in command as to the steps to be taken to prevent disorder and depredations by the Indians and as to the disposition of the troops.
>
> Your acquaintance with the history and the habits and customs of these Indians leads me also to request that you invite statements on their part as to any real or fancied injury or injustice toward them, or any other cause that may have led to discontent, and to inform yourself generally as to their condition. You are justified in assuring them that any cause of complaint will be fully examined by the authorities here, and if wrongs exist they shall be remedied. I think I need hardly add that they must be fully assured of the determination on the part of the Government to enforce their peaceful conduct, and by all the power it has at hand, to prevent and punish acts of lawlessness and any outrage upon our settlers.[5]

Sheridan, an old Indian fighter, reported that the two tribes had been cheated. In July 1885, Cleveland gave the ranchers notice to get themselves and their cattle out of Indian Territory within forty days. Some historians, including Allan Nevins, regard the forty-day deadline as too harsh, though Sheridan had called for quick action in order to avoid major conflict.[6] Since the cattlemen had played fast and loose with truth and honor, the forty-day order does not seem excessively punitive.

Some Indians, Cherokees in particular, had assimilated into white civilization, but most were determined to maintain their traditional way of life. A relatively small population of technologically backward Indians would simply be unable to keep a large part of the continent to itself. The Apache leader Geronimo led the last major attempt by Indians to challenge this reality by waging war on the United States. In September 1886 he surrendered, and the era of Indian independence ended.

To deal with this new situation and encourage the assimilation of Indians, in 1887 Congress passed and Cleveland signed a bill introduced by Senator Henry L. Dawes of Massachusetts that authorized the president to allot tribal land to individual Indians in parcels ranging from 40 to 160 acres. The Indians to whom land was allotted became full American citizens, but they could not sell or encumber their land until twenty-five years had elapsed. Land not allotted to individuals would go into the public domain after payment by the government to the tribe.[7] The long, slow process of acculturation moved ahead.

The clashes between the president and Congress so familiar to Americans today were a fixture of nineteenth-century politics as well. In its drive to politically emasculate President Andrew Johnson during the post–Civil War Reconstruction years, Congress passed the Tenure of Office Act, which required the consent of the Senate to remove any executive officer whose appointment had required Senate confirmation. Congress changed the law in 1869, making it less onerous but not repealing it. Controversy over the law flared up again in Cleveland's first year.

The Senate challenged the president's removal of George M. Duskin, a Republican, as U.S. Attorney for the Southern District of Alabama and his replacement with a Democrat, John D. Burnett, a few months before Duskin's term was to expire. The Senate demanded from Attorney General Garland full documentation of both Duskin's firing and Burnett's nomination. The president directed Garland to provide documentation on the latter but not the former. The Senate objected, demanding all documentation. Cleveland defied the Senate, confident that he was on firm constitutional ground. Looking back on the controversy in 1904, he wrote,

> It seems to me that the gist of the whole matter is contained in a comparison of these two provisions. Under the law of 1867 the incumbent is only conditionally suspended, still having the right to resume his office in case the Senate refuses to concur in the suspension; but under the law of 1869 the Senate had no concern with the suspension of the incumbent, nor with the discretion vested in the President in reference thereto by the express language of the statute; and the suspended incumbent was beyond official resuscitation. Instead of the least intimation that in any event he might "resume the functions of his office," as provided in the law of 1867, it is especially declared that in case the Senate shall refuse to advise and consent to the appointment of the particular person nominated by the President in place of the suspended official, he shall nominate another person to the Senate for such office. Thus the party suspended seems to be eliminated from consideration, the

Senate is relegated to its constitutional rights of confirming or rejecting nominations as it sees fit, and the President is reinstated in his undoubted constitutional power of removal through the form of suspension.[8]

The Senate, in a fighting mood, voted thirty to twenty-five to censure Garland for not turning over all the documents. By then Duskin's term had ended and Burnett was already in office. As there were no grounds for objection to Burnett other than politics, an abashed Senate confirmed him. The next year, 1887, the Tenure of Office Act was repealed in its entirety.

The view that the constitutional separation of church and state requires the expurgation of Christian principles from the law and from public life was still foreign to American thought in Cleveland's day. The president took it for granted that the religious values of the nation were a proper foundation for the nation's laws. The application of Utah for statehood, which raised the question of the legal recognition of polygamy, gave Cleveland an occasion to affirm the moral basis of the law in his first annual message to Congress, on December 8, 1885. The president supported the suppression by law of the polygamy widely practiced by members of the Church of Jesus Christ of Latter-Day Saints, better known as Mormons.

> The strength, the perpetuity, and the destiny of our nation rest upon our homes, established by the law of God, guarded by parental care, regulated by parental authority, and sanctified by parental love.

These are not the homes of polygamy.[9]

A civilized, free society must have a standard by which to determine what is right and what is wrong, Cleveland asserted, confident that his audience would accept his statement for the truism that it was. Cleveland stood on "the law of God," and "God's holy ordinances" as the standard for the United States. These he found in the Bible. In 1890, the Latter-Day Saints repudiated polygamy, and in 1896 Utah was admitted to the Union as the forty-fifth state.

In his personal life, the president soon received the opportunity to practice the monogamous Christian family life that he had extolled. When Cleveland's law partner, Oscar Folsom, was killed in an 1875 accident, he left a widow and an 11-year-old daughter, Frances, but no will. Cleveland was appointed administrator of the estate by the court and did his job well. At some point, as Frances grew up, he started to see the girl in a different light. No longer the sweet little daughter of his late partner, she had grown into a very attractive, vivacious, and intelligent young lady. When Frances entered Wells College[10] in upstate New York, Cleveland, the proper gentleman, sought permission from her mother to write to her. Not surprisingly, permission was granted. Not only was Cleveland a long-time friend of the family, but it would be an unusual mother who would not want a president of the United States as a son-in-law.

Skipping her freshman year, Frances graduated from Wells in 1885 with an excellent academic record. In August, shortly after her graduation, Cleveland proposed to her. She accepted, and the wedding was planned for June of the following year. For now, everything was to be

kept secret. Not long after Frances's acceptance of Cleveland's proposal, she set sail for a tour of Europe with her mother and a male
cousin. The ship's wireless operator copied Cleveland's bon voyage
cable to the ladies and sold it to a New York newspaper. The tone of
the message suggested romance, and the press took it for granted that
the president was courting the widow Folsom. With tongue-in-cheek
outrage, Cleveland complained, "I don't see why the papers keep
marrying me to old ladies. I wonder why they don't say I am engaged
to marry her daughter!"[11]

On May 27, 1886, the Folsom party arrived back in New York.
Daniel Lamont arranged for the two women to leave their liner, board
a tender, and elude the reporters and those curious for a look at the
future "first lady."[12] Cleveland traveled north for Decoration Day
observances in New York and visited briefly with Frances at her hotel
the night before. The following day, as he reviewed parades in Brook-
lyn and Manhattan, bands played Mendelssohn's "Wedding March"
and "He's Going to Marry Yum-Yum" from *The Mikado* by Gilbert
and Sullivan. Then, back to Washington.

The wedding took place on the evening of June 2 in the Blue Room
of the White House with thirty-one guests present. The couple wanted
to avoid the commotion that would have accompanied a church service. The Blue Room was beautifully arrayed with spring flowers. As
Captain John Philip Sousa led the Marine Band in Mendelssohn's
"Wedding March," the couple entered the room. Frances wore a
pearl-white satin gown with a fifteen-foot train. The presiding clergyman was Byron Sunderland, pastor of the Fourth Presbyterian Church,
which Cleveland attended, assisted by the president's brother William,
who pronounced the blessing at the end of the service.[13] After a reception in the East Room and a formal dinner in the State Dining Room,
the couple left by private rail car for a six-day honeymoon in a rented

cottage at Deer Park in the western Maryland mountains. Although the reporters were kept somewhat at bay by security personnel, Cleveland grumbled at the efforts to intrude on his privacy.

The youngest first lady in history (she was twenty-one) and the second to have graduated from college, Frances brought an impressive level of culture to her new position. She was a capable pianist, read Latin, and was fluent in German and French. Her good looks, vivacious personality, and sense of humor made her one of the most adept White House hostesses. She supported educational and professional opportunities for women but did not exploit her position, her favorable press, or her personal popularity. Remarkably level-headed, she kept her focus on her husband and, later, their children. She loved her husband deeply and brightened his life, making him more relaxed and open to the formal social events that were so much a part of official life in Washington. The twenty-seven-year age gap separating Frances and Grover Cleveland was surpassed among presidential couples only by the thirty years separating John Tyler and his second wife. But the difference in age proved to be no obstacle to the happiness and success of their marriage.

The first lady's skill and charm were abundantly displayed at an Executive Mansion reception in the autumn of 1887, attended by Mark Twain. The author was one of the reform-minded, good-government Republicans who had rejected Blaine and supported Cleveland in the 1884 election. Before he left for the reception, Twain's wife slipped a card into his vest pocket reminding him to wear dress shoes. "Don't wear your arctics [snow boots] in the White House," she wrote.[14] After shaking hands with the president, Twain turned to Frances—"the young, the beautiful, the fascinating," he called her[15]— and asked her to sign a card on the back of which he had written, "He didn't." Not understanding why he wanted her to write those words and not wanting to walk into some kind of trap, she demurred. Twain gave her his word that nothing untoward was involved. She signed the card, but warned him, tongue-in-cheek, that: "I will sign it. I will take the risk. But you must tell me all about it, right afterward, so that you can be arrested before you get out of the house in case there should be anything criminal about this."[16]

When Twain showed her his wife's note, she burst out laughing and summoned a messenger to get the card in the mail to the concerned wife, reassuring her that all went well. Cleveland had married well, not just in terms of his personal happiness, but also by having at his side a woman of strength, intelligence, aplomb, and with a sense of fun.

Frances Cleveland was a transitional first lady, bridging the gap between the time when formal education and most professions were closed to women and the present, when educational and professional barriers to the advancement of women have faded. She held two receptions each week, one on Saturday afternoons so that women with jobs could attend. No flaming feminist, no revolutionary, she did advocate change and progress, but within the framework of traditional society. Her husband opposed votes for women. Even though Frances was not part of the women's suffrage movement, it might have been interesting to have eavesdropped on some of their conversations.

Cleveland valued privacy, both for work (long hours dedicated to his duties continued after marriage) and to enjoy his family.[17] He purchased a home on twenty-three acres in the northwestern part of Washington, near where the National Cathedral now stands, an area that was less urbanized than today. Frances named the home Oak View, although it sometimes was called Red Top after Cleveland had the roof painted that color. As much as possible, when the responsibilities of office permitted, the couple lived here.

During these years, the United States economy was growing impressively, opening up opportunities for people at all levels of society. Immigration soared as the combination of political and economic freedom attracted men and women from many countries seeking better lives for themselves and their families. Then as now, however, there were radicals who tried to exploit discontent with the political and economic system's imperfections. The Marxist and anarchist movements of the 1880s opposed improving the system and sought to destroy it instead. Despite economic growth and improved working conditions (the eight-hour day was spreading, and by 1880 only one person in four still worked a ten-hour day[18]), some radical movements flared up.

The Knights of Labor were founded in 1869 as a secret fraternal society that would unite producers, workers, farmers, and shopkeepers. Uriah Stephens, a utopian socialist by conviction, was one of the founders and the first grand master workman. After losing a congressional bid in 1878 as a candidate of the Greenback Labor Party, Stephens resigned as leader of the Knights. Replacing him was Terence Powderly, a railroad worker who joined the organization in 1874 and rose rapidly to the top. He was elected mayor of Scranton, Pennsylvania, three times on the Greenback Labor line. Under Powderly, the Knights ended secrecy, and their membership peaked at seven hundred thousand before falling into rapid decline after 1886.

The brief prominence of the Knights of Labor raised the hopes of the Left and thoroughly alarmed moderates and conservatives. The Knights wanted to abolish private banks, nationalize natural resources, and, in general, replace market capitalism with workers' cooperatives.

In 1885, they enjoyed success striking Jay Gould railroad interests, winning this first round. The next year, though, they overreached, expanding their strikes, hitting more railroads, sabotaging equipment and tracks, and causing deaths. This threat to social order and economic stability turned most of the American public against the Knights, damaged the reputation of the radical movements in general, and provoked a strong response from the states and from the federal government.

Cleveland struck at both sides, assailing the Knights of Labor for resorting to violence and employers for mistreating workers. The president's ability to intervene was limited. The Department of Commerce and Labor was not established until 1903 (Labor became a separate cabinet department in 1913). He called for the creation of a board within the recently established Bureau of Labor to adjudicate disputes, though it would have no binding authority. Congress eventually authorized such a board in 1888.

The most dramatic flare-up of violence was at Haymarket Square in Chicago on May 4, 1886. For several weeks, labor problems, especially at the McCormick Reaper Company, had seethed in the city. Three anarchists—August Spies, Samuel Fielden, and Albert Parsons—took the lead in organizing a protest of workers in Haymarket Square. Initially, everything was peaceful. After rain began, the people started to leave. Police then stepped in to move them along. At that point, someone threw a bomb into the police detachment, cutting down over fifty of them, seven of whom died. The organizers of the rally were tied to the killings and put on trial. Four were hanged, one committed suicide, and three were imprisoned. After seven years, the three survivors were pardoned by Governor John Peter Altgeld. The Haymarket Riot contributed to the polarization of national opinion on labor issues.

A minor appropriation bill passed by Congress in 1887 became the occasion for Cleveland's most famous statement regarding his philosophy of limited government. The Texas Seed Bill provided ten thousand dollars for the purchase of seed grain for farmers in certain Texas counties who had lost crops to drought. The president vetoed the measure with the following statement:

> I can find no warrant for such an appropriation in the Constitution; and I do not believe that the power and duty of the General Government ought to be extended to the relief of individual suffering which is in no manner properly related to the public service or benefit. A prevalent tendency to disregard the limited mission of this power and duty should, I think, be steadily resisted, to the end that the lesson should be constantly enforced that, though the people support the Government, the Government should not support the people.[19]

Conservatives and libertarians may approve the principle that Cleveland expressed so elegantly—that private charity in a low-tax setting is the best way to provide for those in need while preserving a healthy and productive society. It is a measure of the comprehensive triumph of the welfare state, however, that his constitutional scruple over a tiny agricultural appropriation would be nearly incomprehensible to modern Americans.

In the same year, Congress passed the Interstate Commerce Act, prohibiting railroads from charging lower rates to favored customers and from price-fixing. The law's five-member rate-setting board was the first regulatory commission in the history of the federal government. The Constitution plainly empowers Congress to regulate interstate commerce, so this act, though a far greater intrusion on the market than the Texas Seed Bill, encountered no constitutional qualms when it reached the president's desk. Cleveland was troubled by the limited competition and the growth of monopolies in the railroad industry. His support of the Interstate Commerce Act is another example of his determination to preserve freedom from the extremes of exploitation of the people by private interests on the one hand and by government domination on the other.

The amicable partnership known as the "special relationship" between the United States and Great Britain was still decades in the future. The Anglo-American war of the early nineteenth century had established the young republic as a rising force in world affairs, and commercial and military competition, as well as lingering resentments, continued to strain relations between the two English-speaking powers during Cleveland's presidency.

On February 15, 1888, Secretary of State Thomas Bayard and the British foreign secretary, Joseph Chamberlain, signed a treaty that attempted to settle a dispute over Canadian fishing. In July 1885, the U.S. Senate, controlled by Republicans, had abrogated part of an earlier treaty that permitted Canadians to export fish to the United States duty-free in return for allowing Americans to fish in Canadian territorial waters. In retaliation, Canada seized American fishing boats in Canadian waters. In March 1887, Congress passed the Retaliation Act, which authorized the president to bar Canadian ships and products from American ports. The Republicans had a variety of motivations. There was some genuine concern for helping New England fisherman as well as an interest in currying favor with New England voters. Opposition to Britain was thought to attract the votes of traditionally Democratic Irish-Americans. Some senators hoped to appear strong by standing up to the most powerful country in the world, and there were still some who hoped for an opportunity to annex Canada. Cleveland signed the measure but took no action as he worked for a diplomatic resolution of the problems.

The Senate rejected the Bayard-Chamberlain Treaty by a vote of 27 to 30. Cleveland's response showed that while he was a man of principle, he was also a skilled warrior in the jungles of Washington. He called for Congress to give him the power to halt all trade between the United States and Canada. The House complied, but the Republican majority in the Senate recoiled, recognizing that the economic consequences, especially for New England and the Great Lakes states, would be unfavorable. Cleveland had called the Republicans' election-year bluff and forced them to back down. The British observed the terms of the unratified treaty, and the imbroglio faded although tensions continued. Common sense had prevailed, as it would do again in the second Cleveland administration when the United States and Britain clashed over the border between Venezuela and British Guiana. Neither country was a serious threat to the other; they shared too much history and too many common values.

Monetary policy was the subject of ferocious controversy throughout Cleveland's two terms in office, especially the second. Congress had passed the Bland-Allison Act over President Rutherford Hayes's veto in 1878, requiring the United States government to purchase and mint between two and four million dollars' worth of silver each month. This arbitrary increase in the money supply, regardless of economic growth, lowered the value of the dollar and produced inflationary pressures. Hayes and his two immediate successors, James Garfield and Chester Alan Arthur, tried with some success to moderate the inflationary effect of Bland-Allison by purchasing only the minimum amount.

Increasing the money supply seemed like a good idea to many. Debtors could repay what they owed with depreciated dollars. Silver-mining interests and those dependent on them benefitted from Bland-Allison. The most extreme inflationists wanted the government to issue paper money not backed by gold or silver, as it had done during the Civil War, but they could not gain enough support to implement their program. Increasing silver coinage was a way station on their journey to their utopian left-wing society.

Cleveland was convinced of the validity of Gresham's Law,[20] that overvalued money drives undervalued money out of circulation. Generally the silver value of coins was less than the official value, whereas the opposite was true of gold coins. As a result, people spent the silver and hoarded the gold. In February 1885, shortly before Cleveland was inaugurated, Democratic Representative Abram Hewitt of New York, the chairman of the House Ways and Means Committee, introduced a bill to stop the coinage of silver, but it was defeated by a coalition of 118 Democrats and 52 Republicans.

Despite setback, Cleveland did what he could to oppose inflationary monetary policies, reversing the Arthur administration's policy of redeeming bonds in gold. As a result, gold holdings increased and monetary stability ensued. Later, in 1885, he called in vain for Congress to repeal Bland-Allison. The rest of his term saw a stand-off between the sound-money side and those who believed inflation of the money supply would bring prosperity.

During his first term, Cleveland filled two vacancies on the Supreme Court. In 1888, he nominated Secretary of the Interior Lucius Lamar, reviving the furious opposition that had accompanied Lamar's appointment to the cabinet. Lamar's opponents pointed to his support for secession three decades earlier, his service in the Confederate army, and his age (sixty-two). Lamar won his seat on the bench by a close 32 to 28 vote in the Senate. His strict interpretation of the Constitution was in line with Cleveland's, but his death in 1893 cut short his influence.

In the same year, Cleveland nominated Melville W. Fuller as the new chief justice. Born in Maine, Fuller graduated from Bowdoin College, studied law at Harvard, then moved to Illinois, where he practiced law and served one term in the U.S. House of Representatives. A conservative Democrat, he opposed slavery and secession but criticized the Lincoln administration for aggressive tactics like suspending habeas corpus. His conservatism was also expressed by his support of sound money. Fuller was an effective chief justice, holding office from 1888 to 1910 and proving himself adept at building a consensus among his colleagues. Justice Oliver Wendell Holmes Jr., whom Theodore Roosevelt appointed in 1902, considered Fuller the best chief justice he had ever known.

Like most Americans, Cleveland had little interest in projecting the power of the United States beyond North America. Despite some interest in the Pacific and in Central America, along with antipathy to Spanish rule in Cuba, there was little support for active involvement in overseas affairs. The British Empire was the most powerful political force in the world, about one-fourth of the earth's surface being under the Union Jack. Despite occasional tensions, America did not regard Britain as a threat. The French empire was important but trailed the British in extent and power. It also was not considered a threat to American interests. Germany was a different case. During the latter part of the nineteenth century, the Germans had grown more powerful in Europe and striven to develop an empire in Africa and in the Pacific. Germany was new to empire-building and was determined to make up for its late start. It had united in 1871, had industrialized rapidly, and was moving to become the preeminent power in Europe while simultaneously challenging Britain around the world.

Japan had not yet flexed its muscles and launched its imperial expansion during Cleveland's first administration, but the rise of Japan was not far in the future. In the middle of the nineteenth century, the Japanese had commenced the modernization of their economy and of their armed forces. They learned much from the West—the British navy and the German army were exemplars for them—but they remained cautious, firmly Japanese, avoiding the cultural and economic imperialism to which China had been subjected. Japan soon would begin its own imperialistic expansion. The Sino-Japanese War of 1894–1895 would leave Japan in control of Taiwan and Korea. Further probing of the mainland would follow, leading in 1904 to war with Russia, a country extending its influence into the same area at the same time as well as expanding its influence in Europe and in the Middle East. Japan also turned its attention eastward as far as the then-independent Hawaii, where a good number of its citizens had emigrated.

The completion of the transcontinental railroad in 1869 led to the growth of America's west-coast ports and the expansion of trade with Australia, New Zealand, and Asia. During the administrations of Hayes, Garfield, and Arthur, therefore, interest started to grow in acquiring coaling stations and naval bases for the protection of American trade.

Samoa, an independent monarchy in the southwest Pacific, had been visited by Europeans in the early eighteenth century. Christian missionary activity in the first half of the next century was successful. Concerned that British and German influence would restrict American trade in the region, the Hayes administration signed a treaty with Samoa in 1878, giving the U.S. the use of the Pago Pago harbor as a fueling station for naval and commercial ships. The United States agreed to mediate disputes between Samoa and other countries, and Samoa agreed that Americans there would be judged by American law. The United States, the United Kingdom, and Germany all agreed to respect Samoan sovereignty. Samoa's geographical importance, however, and the continued expansion of the German empire eventually doomed prospects for amity.

Five years later, Germany struck, sending a naval force to Samoa and then supporting a revolt against its king, Malietoa. Citing the 1878 treaty, the king appealed to the United States for help. Cleveland, newly in office, called for peaceful adjudication and for the three powers to respect Samoan sovereignty. Germany officially supported a three-party conference while working covertly for German control. A conference in Washington in 1887 accomplished nothing. The British, though they opposed German expansion, had decided that their best course was to work out spheres of influence; Samoa would be left to Germany. When the Germans then moved to solidify their domination, Cleveland reacted strongly, informing Germany that he stood on the three-party agreement and would not tolerate German aggression. Cleveland preferred a non-interventionist foreign policy, but he reacted decisively when U.S. interests were under assault and when a small country within the area of American national interest was threatened by a powerful adversary. The German government was informed that the United States would not tolerate a German takeover of Samoa. Exactly how Cleveland might back up the threat was not specified, but the clear implication was that intervention by American armed forces was a distinct possibility.

The Germans, feeling secure in their understanding with the British, did not believe that Cleveland would do anything beyond blustering, so they overthrew Malietoa in 1888 and replaced him with their puppet. They had misread Cleveland. He ordered a naval ship to Samoa, where there already were four German vessels. The American action encouraged the native Samoans to overthrow the German puppet government, an outcome Germany was not prepared to accept.

The year 1888 ended with Samoa simmering. Meanwhile, Cleveland lost his race for reelection to Benjamin Harrison.[21] The new president was determined to maintain the strong American position and sent three warships to Samoa. Before warfare could break out, however, a massive typhoon struck on March 16, sinking both the American and the German ships. The situation in Samoa quieted down, and diplomacy again came to the fore. Finally, in 1899, the islands were divided between the United States and Germany.[22]

There is a final story to tell—perhaps apocryphal—about Grover Cleveland's first term as president. In 1887, five-year-old Franklin Delano Roosevelt accompanied his father, James, a prominent member of the Hudson River gentry, on a visit to the president. Although a Cleveland supporter, James Roosevelt had declined an appointment as ambassador to the Netherlands, as he had earlier rejected suggestions that he run for Congress or for the state legislature. Cleveland is said to have patted the boy on the head and said, "My little man, I am making a strange wish for you. It is that you may never be president of the United States."[23] Whether the story is true or not, there is many a conservative who regrets that Cleveland's wish did not come true.

~⚜ CHAPTER 5 ⚜~

DEFEAT AND INTERREGNUM

WITH THE ARRIVAL OF 1888, another presidential campaign season began. The Democrats met first, opening their national convention in St. Louis on June 5. There was no organized opposition to a second term for Cleveland.[1] The vice presidency had been vacant since Thomas Hendricks had died less than a year into his term.[2] The convention nominated Allen G. Thurman of Ohio to be Cleveland's running mate in 1888. A former U.S. representative and senator, Thurman had narrowly lost a gubernatorial race against Rutherford B. Hayes two decades earlier and enjoyed a reputation for integrity and ability. Ohio was a large state and crucial to the electoral prospects of both parties. Thurman, who was seventy-five and in less than robust health, did not share Cleveland's views on monetary and tariff policy.

The Republicans opened their national convention in Chicago on June 19. James G. Blaine had removed himself from consideration because of poor health. The most prominent alternative to Blaine was

Senator John Sherman of Ohio, the secretary of the Treasury in the Hayes administration and the brother of General William Tecumseh Sherman. Other prominent contenders were Chauncey Depew of New York and Walter Q. Gresham of Indiana. Depew had started as a lawyer for the Vanderbilt railroad interests, advanced to be president of the New York Central and Hudson River Railroad, and eventually became the chairman of the entire Vanderbilt system. Gresham, also an attorney, served as a brevet major general during the Civil War, as a federal circuit judge, and as both postmaster general and secretary of the Treasury under President Arthur.

In case none of these men could win enough delegates for victory, Benjamin Harrison of Indiana was poised to enter the contest. A great-grandson of Benjamin Harrison, a signer of the Declaration of Independence, a grandson of President William Henry Harrison, and a son of U.S. Representative John Scott Harrison, he had a formidable political pedigree. He graduated from Miami University in Ohio, became a lawyer, and served bravely and capably during the Civil War, rising to the rank of brigadier general. Harrison lost a bid for the governorship of Indiana in 1876, was elected to the U.S. Senate in 1881, but was defeated narrowly for a second term. He was small and lacking in personal warmth, but possessed outstanding oratorical skill. His popularity among veterans, advocacy of high tariffs, and close relations with party leaders made him an attractive candidate, and he came from an important swing state.

When the balloting began, Sherman surged into the lead but fell short of the requisite number of votes to be the nominee. For three ballots this deadlock continued. Gresham and Depew could not catch Sherman, let alone win the nomination. Governor Russell Alger of Michigan rose on the third ballot then faded. The attempts to propel Gresham, Depew, and Alger ahead of Sherman had foundered, and

Harrison's moment had come. On the fourth ballot he shot up to second place, moved into first place on the seventh, and won on the eighth. His running mate was Levi Morton of New York, who had declined James Garfield's invitation to be his running mate in 1880. A wealthy banker who had served in the House of Representatives and as minister to France, Morton became the governor of New York after his term as vice president.

The presidential election of 1888 was a relatively dull affair, lacking charismatic candidates or sharp differences between the parties on momentous issues. The two nominees were intelligent, capable men of integrity, and they both refrained from vigorous personal campaigning. Cleveland believed that the president should be above the fray and that his record spoke for itself. Harrison confined himself to meeting delegations at his Indianapolis home and addressing audiences from his front porch. Fighting in the trenches was left to subordinates.

The most important issue was the tariff. While rejecting absolute free trade, Cleveland favored lowering the rates, arguing that high duties raised prices at home and resulted in retaliation by other countries. Harrison argued that low tariffs harmed American businesses and resulted in lower wages for American workers, but he did not emphasize the issue. The Republicans called for civil rights for black citizens in the South, a position that kept white voters in that region solidly in the Democratic camp despite strong protectionist sentiment in the iron-mining parts of Tennessee, Alabama, and West Virginia, in the sugar-growing region of Louisiana, and in the few industrial areas of the South. Four years later, there would be more contentious issues, making the 1892 race more exciting by far.

For Cleveland, his home state of New York, with its thirty-six electoral votes, was once again the key to victory. Complicating Cleveland's prospects was the presence of David Hill as governor. Though

Hill, out of self-interest, expressed support for his party's ticket, Cleveland refused to support the reelection of the governor, whom he considered lacking in honor and integrity. Officially, Cleveland simply affirmed that the president should not try to influence state politics, and he took no position in the gubernatorial race.

Hill's organization, as a consequence, did little to help Cleveland carry New York, while working assiduously for the governor. The president failed to carry New York, and from Hill's perspective, the election produced the best result possible—Hill's reelection and Cleveland's defeat. The presidency, Hill believed, was now within reach.

Benjamin Harrison carried twenty states with 233 electoral votes, while Cleveland carried eighteen states with 168 electoral votes. A shift of 14,000 votes in New York would have returned Cleveland to what soon would officially be called the White House. The national popular vote, however, went to Cleveland 5,540,329 to 5,439,853, making him one of only three men in American history to win the popular vote while losing in the Electoral College.[3]

As might be expected, recriminations followed this narrow defeat. Some argued that Cleveland should have avoided bringing up the tariff controversy in an election year. It can also be argued that he ought to have started the debate earlier so the administration could counter the Republican charges of business failure and job losses. Certainly the case is stronger that the Democratic campaign suffered from the inept leadership of Calvin Brice, that energy and effectiveness were absent. Cleveland made a mistake by agreeing to Brice, later national chairman of the party and a member of the U.S. Senate. Thurman pushed Brice as a moderate on the tariff who would deflect Republican charges that the Democrats wanted free trade. In the name of party unity, Cleveland accepted Brice.

From the vantage point of today, things that Cleveland should have done differently are evident. In any case, Cleveland refused to look back. He was stubborn, but he did not become bitter or depressed over the outcome of the election. He had fought to win. Now he accepted his loss with grace and got on with his life.

On December 8, Cleveland sent his fourth annual message to Congress. With no plans for mounting a political comeback, he saw this message as his last major opportunity to address the nation as chief executive. His assessment of the state of the country was generally positive, but he did express concern over a perceived polarization of American society:

> The gulf between employers and the employed is constantly widening, and classes are rapidly forming, one comprising the very rich and powerful, while in another are the toiling poor.... We discover the existence of trusts, combinations, and monopolies, while the citizen is struggling far in the rear or is trampled to death beneath an iron heel.[4]

Cleveland was always a limited-government conservative, but he understood clearly that a free market requires a foundation in moral principles. He was coming to recognize the growing threat to justice and freedom from concentrated wealth unrestrained by integrity. Though he never wavered from his belief in free markets, he became convinced of the need for the federal government's intervention in economic matters in order to preserve the freedom of the market.

On March 4, 1889, in the middle of an inauspicious thunderstorm, Benjamin Harrison was sworn in as the twenty-third president. Frances Cleveland is said to have admonished the staff of the White House that day to take good care of everything since the Clevelands would be back in four years.[5] She was remarkably prescient or determined, or perhaps she was simply confronting disappointment with a bold face.

Cleveland sold his private residence, Oak View, for a $100,000 profit and moved to New York City to begin the next phase of his life. He had saved about $25,000 each year as president—roughly half his salary—and although he was by no means rich, he was financially comfortable.[6] He needed to earn a living, but he needed even more to be productive.

A good number of prestigious law firms were eager to add the former president's name to their letterhead. His friendship with Francis Lynde Stetson of Bangs, Stetson, Tracy & MacVeigh, one of the preeminent firms in the country,[7] was decisive, and he became "of counsel" with the firm, meaning that he did not share in the profits and did not contribute to the expenses of the practice.

Cleveland had a suite of offices and a staff. He was much sought after as a referee in complicated cases, and his firm's partners frequently consulted with him. He continued, as in his previous law practices, to do his own research and write his own briefs.

He still worked hard during the day, but no longer did his practice absorb much of his nights. Now financially secure and with a family,[8] home life and vacations were a major part of his life. Shortly after leaving the presidency, Cleveland rented a four-story brownstone on Madison Avenue near Sixty-Eighth Street. The Clevelands partook of the New York night life to a limited extent, but generally preferred quiet nights at home together or with a few friends.

During his first summer out of office, Cleveland accepted an invitation from Richard Watson Gilder, editor of the *Century* (a monthly magazine), to visit him at his Cape Cod summer home. The Clevelands then rented a nearby cottage on Buzzards Bay. The next summer, they again rented, and in 1891 purchased, a house called Gray Gables. Waterfront, several acres of woods, and the six miles between the house and the nearest railroad station gave the family its needed privacy. Cleveland enjoyed the company of friends, including the actor Joseph Jefferson, the publisher William Appleton, and the attorney Richard Olney, who had a summer home in Falmouth,[9] a few miles south of Gray Gables. Fishing and visiting with neighborhood children helped the former president relax in preparation for a return to the political arena.

At first Cleveland seemed really to have retired from political combat. But several developments drew him back into the fray and fueled interest across the country in another Cleveland presidency.

With control of the White House and both houses of Congress, the Republicans enacted several controversial measures. Pension spending increased sharply with the passage of a bill in 1890 extending coverage to any Civil War veteran who was incapable of working, even if the disability had nothing to do with his service.

Also enacted in 1890 was the McKinley Tariff. Introduced by Representative William McKinley of Ohio, it was the highest peacetime tariff in American history up to that time, and it produced a sharp increase in consumer prices. In the era before the federal income tax, the government's revenue came primarily from two sources—tariffs levied on imports (60 percent of the total) and internal taxes on certain items, especially tobacco and whiskey. When Harrison took office, the tariff was generating a substantial surplus—$105 million at a time when government expenditures amounted to only $282 million.[10] In November, a majority of the voters would leave no doubt as to their displeasure over the high tariff rates.

In 1889 and 1890, six new states entered the union—North Dakota, South Dakota, Montana, Washington, Idaho, and Wyoming. These states favored the silverite position of increasing the coinage of silver to aid silver-mining interests and to inflate the money supply. The additional votes in Congress enabled the silver party to pass the Sherman Silver Purchase Act. Bearing the name of Senator John Sherman of Ohio, the bill was designed to draw support from both Republicans and Democrats in Congress. It did, and the amount of silver purchased by the government each month went up dramatically. The supporters of the McKinley Tariff and the supporters of the Sherman Silver Purchase Act were not natural allies, but a quid pro quo was worked out, and each group got what it most wanted.

Now the purchase of 4.5 million ounces of silver per month was mandated, roughly double of the amount purchased under Bland-Allison. The silver was paid for with paper currency redeemable in either gold or silver. Those with foresight chose gold rather than the increasingly depreciated silver, and many who had held silver exchanged it for gold, resulting in a serious depletion of government gold holdings. This economic uncertainty eroded public confidence in the Harrison administration, and the November 1890 election produced a sharp change in direction. The Democrats gained two Senate seats, though the Republicans retained control of the chamber. But the House saw one of the most stunning reversals in the history of congressional elections. The House elected in 1888 had 166 Republicans and 159 Democrats. The 1890 election gave the Democrats a margin of 235 to 88, with nine seats held by third parties.

Early in 1891, Cleveland spoke to the members of the Young Men's Democratic Association of Philadelphia at their yearly Jackson Day dinner. He offered a vision that was not merely exalted rhetoric, but expressed his deepest convictions. He titled his address "The Principles of True Democracy," which he described as follows:

> Equal and exact justice to all men, peace, commerce, and honest friendship with all nations—entangling alliance with none; the support of the State governments in all their rights; the preservation of the general government in its whole constitutional vigor; a jealous care of the right of election by the people; absolute acquiescence in the decisions of the majority; the supremacy of the civil over the military authority; economy in the public expenses; the honest payment of our debts and sacred preservation of the public faith; the encouragement of agriculture, and commerce as its handmaid, and freedom of religion, freedom of the press, and freedom of the person.[11]

He condemned the growth in government spending, which is not only wasteful of taxpayers' money but leads to dependency:

> When we see the extravagance of public expenditure fast reaching the point of reckless waste, and the undeserved

distribution of public money debauching its recipients, and
by pernicious example threatening the destruction of the
love of frugality among our people, we will remember that
"economy in the public expense is an important article in
the true Democratic faith."[12]

Cleveland's insistence on "absolute acquiescence in the decisions of
the majority" was perhaps a slightly hyperbolic expression of his belief
in free elections, but his record does not support the view that he was
a democratic absolutist. The divine law was the foundation of human
law, in Cleveland's view, and was not subject to the will of the majority. Almost everyone alive at the end of the nineteenth century would
have shared this view, however exotic it may seem in our own rela-
tivistic age.

He went on to describe a government modest in its scope but
vigorous in the execution of its duties, especially the defense of justice:

It is right that every man should enjoy the result of his labor
to the fullest extent consistent with his membership in
civilized community. It is right that our government should
be but the instrument of the people's will, and that its cost
should be limited within the lines of strict economy. It is
right that the influence of the government should be known
in every humble home as the guardian of frugal comfort
and content, and a defense against unjust exactions, and
the unearned tribute persistently coveted by the selfish and
designing. It is right that efficiency and honesty in public
service should not be sacrificed to partisan greed; and it is
right that the suffrage of our people should be pure and
free.[13]

Early in the following year, on Washington's birthday, the former president returned to the theme of good government in a speech to students at the University of Michigan. Cleveland again affirmed his belief that the decrees of God are never out of date and that this country has been blessed richly by Him. While acknowledging the military skill, fortitude, and statesmanship of the first president, Cleveland reminded the students that Washington's greatness rested above all on his devotion to high principles.

> You may be chosen to public office. Do not shrink from it, for holding office is also a duty of citizenship. But do not leave your faith behind you. Every public office, small or great, is held in trust for your fellow-citizens. They differ in importance, in responsibility, and in the labor they impose; but the duties of none of them can be well performed if the mentorship of a good conscience and pure heart be discarded. Of course, other equipment is necessary, but without this mentorship all else is insufficient. In times of gravest responsibility it will solve your difficulties; in the most trying hour it will lead you out of perplexities, and it will, at all times, deliver you from temptation.
>
> In conclusion, let me remind you that we may all properly learn the lesson appropriate to Washington's birthday, if we will; and that we shall fortify ourselves against the danger.[14]

ஜ CHAPTER 6 ஜ

BACK INTO
THE ARENA

B Y EARLY 1892, IT was clear that a rejuvenated Cleveland was emerging from retirement. There was rejoicing among those who favored sound, honest, limited government, but the return of Grover Cleveland was a blow to Governor David Hill's plans to seize the leadership of the Democratic Party and claim the presidency for himself.

The Republican National Convention met in June in Minneapolis. There was little enthusiasm for Benjamin Harrison, but no good alternative. After having removed himself from consideration four years earlier, James G. Blaine bestirred himself for a "last hurrah." He had the support of some party leaders, such as House speaker Thomas Reed, but not much among the party rank and file. Harrison won the nomination on the first ballot, receiving 535 1/6 votes, swamping Blaine's 182 5/6 and William McKinley's 182.

Two weeks later, the Democrats convened in Chicago. Cleveland also was nominated on the first ballot, but there were more fireworks here than in Minneapolis. Hill's machinations had alienated most of the party faithful, who saw him as an unprincipled schemer. On the first ballot in Chicago, Cleveland received 617 ½ votes (ten more than needed), Hill 114, Governor Horace Boies of Iowa 103, and the remainder scattered. It was clear to most of the delegates that not only was Cleveland the best candidate, but also the only one likely to defeat Harrison.

Cleveland's running mate was Adlai Stevenson of Illinois, grandfather of the Adlai Stevenson who would lose the 1952 and 1956 presidential elections to Dwight Eisenhower. A former member of the House of Representatives and an assistant postmaster general in Cleveland's first term, Stevenson was nominated to placate the free-silver wing of the party. The platform tried to skirt the issue of silver, though Cleveland himself did not. It also called for a tariff for revenue only, not for the protection of industry. The platform advocated anti-trust legislation and federal assistance to education in rather general terms, a canal across Central America, and Irish home rule.

Cleveland's campaign manager, the former secretary of the navy William C. Whitney of New York, persuaded him to make New York Lieutenant Governor William Sheehan his campaign committee chairman for the state. Sheehan, a Tammany man, met with Cleveland and demanded that he stop pro-Cleveland newspapers from attacking Tammany and insisted on more patronage from a new Cleveland administration. Demanding that he do something was never the way to succeed with Grover Cleveland, and Sheehan's affiliation with Tammany only darkened his prospects. Cleveland's response was audacious and devastating:

> I will appeal from the machine to the people. This very
> night I will issue a declaration to the electors of the state

telling them the proposition you have made to me and the reasons why I am not able to accept it. I will ask them to choose between us. Such is my confidence in the people that before the week ends, I believe that your machine will be in revolution against you.[1]

Tammany, including Sheehan and Hill, backed down and supported Cleveland on his terms. Sheehan ought to have known that Cleveland would be impervious to intimidation. He would not sacrifice principle in order to win an election.

The election of 1892 did not present voters a simple choice between the Republicans and the Democrats. Harrison and Cleveland were both conservative, Cleveland more so. Those on the Left felt disenfranchised and coalesced into the People's Party, more commonly known as the Populist Party. Its presidential candidate was James B. Weaver of Iowa, an attorney and an early member of the Republican Party. During the Civil War, he served in the Union army, rising to the rank of brigadier general. His positions in favor of free silver and prohibition, however, put him outside the Republican mainstream, and his postwar career with the party was brief. Gravitating to the Greenback Party, he was elected to three terms in the House of Representatives, serving from 1879 to 1881 and from 1885 to 1889. In 1880, as the Greenback nominee for president, he received 308,000 votes, 3.35 percent of the total. Seeking a national unity ticket, the Populists chose the Confederate veteran James G. Field of Virginia as his running mate. The Populists staked out a position distinctly to the left of the two major parties, adopting a platform of unlimited coinage of silver; government ownership of railroad, telephone, and telegraph companies; savings banks operated by the Post Office; and a graduated income tax. They also called for the direct election of United

States senators, a one-term limit for presidents, and the introduction of initiative, referendum, and recall elections at the federal level.

In late June and early July, just after the Republican and Democratic conventions, one of the most famous and most dramatic labor disputes in American history took place: the strike of the Amalgamated Association of Iron and Steel Workers against the Carnegie Steel Company in Homestead, Pennsylvania, a short distance from Pittsburgh. The union, which was part of the American Federation of Labor headed by Samuel Gompers, had won recognition along with wage and working-hours concessions from other companies in the area. Now, however, it confronted a tougher, more resolute foe determined not just to resist the union's demands but to eliminate it. Andrew Carnegie entrusted the Homestead mill operations to Henry Clay Frick, who had achieved great success on his own developing coal fields and building coke ovens before joining the more powerful Carnegie empire. Preparing for the trouble to come, Frick hired three hundred Pinkerton Detective Agency men to be the hard core of his campaign to break the union's power. The strikers also were armed. Trouble was not long in coming.

On July 6, a force of strikers fired on a barge carrying the Pinkerton men to the plant on the Monongahela River. The strikers even had two small cannon. Ten Pinkerton men were killed and over sixty wounded. The rest surrendered and were permitted to leave. The governor of Pennsylvania, Robert E. Pattison, now ordered eight thousand state militiamen to Homestead to restore order and protect the plant. Public opinion, which supported the principle of collective bargaining and opposed strike-breakers, turned against the union in the wake of its violence, and most of its workers quit. Carnegie and Frick had prevailed. Cleveland, as always, called for law and order but deplored the lowering of wages in the aftermath of the strike and castigated businessmen who exploited their employees and thus abused the free enterprise system.

Other labor disputes during the election season increased problems for the Republicans. Silver miners in Coeur d'Alene, Idaho, responded to wage cuts by seizing the mine and expelling the nonunion workers hired to replace them. Harrison sent in the army to restore order. In Buffalo, the state militia could not handle a strike by railroad employees, and once again army units did the job. Those who favored these union actions were determined to retaliate politically against Harrison.

Compared with earlier and later presidential campaigns, the 1892 contest was mild. Cleveland held to his earlier practice of making few appearances, letting his record and surrogates make the case to the voting public. Some episodes of gout reinforced this policy, and he spent much of the time after the national convention at Gray Gables.

The Democratic Party was rent by deep fissures over monetary policy and the tariff. The first was mended, tenuously, by the ticket of Cleveland, a gold-standard advocate, and Stevenson, a silverite. The dispute over tariffs was subordinated, also tenuously, in the name of party unity, although Cleveland's low tariff stance was well known. These two issues, especially the first, would make it extraordinarily difficult for Cleveland to unite the party after the election and foreshadowed the split in 1896 that produced almost a generation of Republican domination. Alyn Brodsky insightfully writes that three paths lay before Cleveland. First, he could have been a weak president, avoiding decisive action. The second alternative was to attempt some type of compromise. The third choice was to stand firmly on his principles even though controversy and division would follow. Cleveland, of course, took the third path.[2]

Brodsky, who admires Cleveland's principles, faults him for wanting to show "how forceful and principled he could be, instead of how unifying."[3] That last statement could be unfair to Cleveland. There is no question that he was principled and determined, but it is hard to see how the Democrats could have avoided the reefs that lay ahead after the election. For now, though, prospects were bright for Cleveland and his party, especially in view of the immediate problems that inundated Harrison and the Republicans.

Harrison had to bear the brunt of labor's ire over the failure of the Homestead strike. His running mate, Whitelaw Reid, the publisher and editor of the *New York Tribune*, had had a labor dispute of his own, which antagonized those sympathetic to workers. The labor movement, moreover, was coming to see that it had not benefited from the high tariff as the Republicans had said it would. This also hurt Harrison.

Farmers who wanted the unlimited coinage of silver saw neither Cleveland nor Harrison as favorable to their cause and turned increasingly to Weaver and the Populists. Hoping to stem the flow of support to the Populists, Harrison tried to adopt a position which would placate both the hard-money and the soft-money interests. He satisfied neither. The most committed hard-money people favored Cleveland, and the soft-money voters preferred Weaver.

Divided as they were, the Democrats were nevertheless more united than the Republicans. For example, the prominent silverite Senator Daniel W. Voorhees of Indiana strongly endorsed Cleveland. Supporting Cleveland from the other direction was the Republican Walter Q. Gresham, who had been postmaster general and secretary of the Treasury under Arthur and a contender for the Republican presidential nomination in 1888. Agreeing with Cleveland on monetary policy and on the tariff, he broke with his party and backed Cleveland. Republican hopes were further undermined by personal spats. Thomas Reed, the once and future speaker of the House, for example, was alienated from his party leaders over patronage disputes.

The sometimes brilliant and generally acerbic Henry Adams, the great-grandson of John Adams, preferred Cleveland to Harrison for his own quirky reasons. In his third-person memoir, Adams recalled,

> Mr. Harrison was an excellent President, a man of ability and force; perhaps the best President the Republican Party had put forward since Lincoln's death; yet, on the whole, Adams felt a shade of preference for President Cleveland, not so much personally as because the Democrats represented to him the last remnants of the eighteenth century; the survivors of Hosea Biglow's Cornwallis; the sole remaining protestants against a banker's Olympus which had become, for five-and-twenty years, more and more despotic over Esop's [sic] frog-empire.[4]

Harrison was distracted from the campaign by the failing health of his wife, Caroline. She was belatedly diagnosed in the middle of September with tuberculosis. A little over a month later, on October 25, she died. This ended campaigning by Harrison and, out of respect for the president's loss, Cleveland suspended what little active involvement he had planned in the contest over the final two weeks.

The Democratic Party decided not to enter slates of electors in several western states where the Populists were strong—Idaho, Colorado, Wyoming, North Dakota, and Kansas—further diminishing Republican prospects. Even if the Democrats could not win these states, they could deprive Harrison of their electoral votes.

Cleveland and the Democrats won handily on Election Day, taking twenty-three states with 277 electoral votes. Harrison carried sixteen states with 145 electoral votes. Weaver won four states with twenty electoral votes and one elector each from Oregon and North Dakota. Cleveland's popular vote margin was not as overwhelming but still substantial: 5,556,918—46 percent of the votes cast. Harrison was the choice of 5,176,108—43 percent of the votes. Weaver got 1,041,028 votes—9 percent. These were results to please any conservative. Grover Cleveland now had made his mark in American history as the only person to have won the presidency, lost his bid for reelection, and won a rematch. Also, Cleveland had won the popular vote in three consecutive presidential elections, the only man other than Franklin Roosevelt ever to do so. After a four-year hiatus, the Clevelands moved back to Washington.

⁓⚜ CHAPTER 7 ⚜⁓

SECOND TERM

O N MARCH 4, 1893, Cleveland once more took office as president of the United States. The oath was administered by Chief Justice Melville W. Fuller, whom Cleveland had nominated in his first term. His left hand again rested on the Bible his mother had given him, which was open to Psalm 91:12: "They shall bear thee up in their hands, lest thou dash thy foot against a stone."[1] The delightful weather of his first inauguration was replaced by snow and freezing rain, auguring the stormy days that lay ahead in the second term.

The hardy audience was no doubt relieved that the president's address was shorter than the recent norm,[2] although it was longer than his first. Cleveland did not chart a bold course of dramatically new policies. Instead, he called for renewed and strengthened adherence to sound principles. Strong and stable money, he affirmed, was essential for the economy to function well and for the country to be healthy. The drift away from the gold standard represented by the

Sherman Silver Purchase Act should be halted. He called for low tariffs, fairness for American Indians, careful screening of Civil War veterans' pensions. As always, Cleveland insisted on limited government, frugality, and low taxes.

The returning president warned of the danger of government paternalism, which seductively undermines citizens' self-reliance and thus their freedom. His admonition that "while the people should patriotically and cheerfully support their government, its functions do not include the support of the people"[3] encapsulated his political philosophy, making clear beyond the shadow of a doubt his commitment to limited government, a commitment that would soon come under assault from the left wing of Cleveland's own party.

The president's address concluded with an affirmation of the country's reliance on divine providence:

> Above all, I know there is a Supreme Being who rules the affairs of men and whose goodness and mercy have always followed the American people, and I know He will not turn from us now if we humbly and reverently seek His powerful aid.[4]

For the first time since the Buchanan administration in the 1850s, the Democrats controlled both houses of Congress. The voters' confidence in Cleveland, regarded as a man of integrity, courage, and ability, was high, and it transcended differences over specific issues such as monetary policy and the tariff.

Cleveland again selected a cabinet of capable men who shared his views of domestic and foreign policy. Some historians are dismissive

of his cabinet. H. Paul Jeffers quotes Richard E. Welch Jr., who sees
it as an echo chamber for the president's unchallenged views:

> Although it was not a strong cabinet, it would prove to be
> a loyal and unified cabinet. In his official family, Cleveland
> would find the solace of agreement and friendship, but he
> would receive no criticism or correction when those offer-
> ings might have served him better than unanimity. Few of
> its members had played an important role in party politics,
> and they would have little influence with party members
> in Congress. In the coming battles over the currency and
> the tariff, they would not be able to furnish the political
> finesse their chief both lacked and disdained.[5]

Welch's characterization of the cabinet is unfair. This was no collection
of ciphers. Cleveland's cabinet included men of strong character who
had made their mark in the world, even if they had not "played an
important role in party politics" (though some of them had). It is by
no means clear that more "political finesse" could have staved off the
rise of William Jennings Bryan and the populist wing of the Democratic
Party. Outside of the East, most of the party faithful soon succumbed
to the seductive call for cheap money and more government.

Heading the cabinet as secretary of state was the former Republican and sometime presidential contender Walter Q. Gresham of
Indiana, who broke with his party because he believed strongly in low
tariff rates and more civil service reform.

John G. Carlisle of Kentucky, the former speaker of the House,
was Cleveland's choice to head the Treasury Department. His advocacy of the gold standard and of lower tariffs made him the target of
the increasingly assertive left wing of his party.

Richard Olney of Massachusetts became the new attorney general. An intelligent, tough, and successful attorney, his experience in the public sector was limited to a single term in the Massachusetts legislature. He would make his mark both as attorney general and, in a couple years, as secretary of state.

The new secretary of the navy was Hilary A. Herbert of Alabama, a former colonel in the Confederate army who had been severely wounded in action. A lawyer, he served eight terms in the U.S. House of Representatives, where he rose to be chairman of the naval affairs committee. A longtime proponent of naval expansion, he continued and expanded the work of Benjamin Tracy, his predecessor in the Harrison administration. Herbert would be remembered as one of the most important secretaries of the navy.

Cleveland selected his right-hand man from New York and his private secretary during his first term, Daniel S. Lamont, to be secretary of war. The new postmaster general was another New York associate, Cleveland's old friend and former law partner Wilson S. Bissell.

Hoke Smith of Georgia came in as secretary of the interior. Too young to have fought in the Civil War, he was an attorney, owner of the *Atlanta Journal*, and later governor of Georgia and a United States senator. The secretary of agriculture was J. Sterling Morton of Nebraska, the founder of Arbor Day. Before the explosion of the welfare state, this cabinet officer's job primarily entailed promoting agricultural exports.

Once again, the paths of Grover Cleveland and Theodore Roosevelt crossed. President Harrison had appointed Roosevelt to the three-man Civil Service Commission, which had been established under the Pendleton Act. Roosevelt, who had been frustrated by the Harrison administration's lack of interest in civil service reform, was

surprised when Cleveland retained him on the commission. When
Cleveland had been governor of New York and Roosevelt the Republican leader in the assembly, they had cooperated, then split. Cleveland, though, bore no grudge and agreed with Roosevelt on the need
for civil service reform. They now worked together for two years until
Roosevelt resigned to accept appointment as police commissioner for
New York City.

On February 20, a few days before the new administration took
office, the Philadelphia and Reading Railway collapsed, a harbinger
of the Panic of 1893 and a year of extraordinary challenge for Cleveland. When he returned to office on March 4, the government's gold
reserve, which had risen from $125 million to almost $200 million
during his first term, had fallen to an historic low of just under $101
million. Working through the secretary of the Treasury, Cleveland was
able to persuade key bankers to purchase currency with gold and thus
evaded the immediate threat to the strength and stability of the dollar.
The gold reserve soon increased to $107 million. This relief, though,
was short-lived, for the causes of the crisis went back years.

For decades prior to 1893, the United States had struggled to
maintain "bimetallism," meaning that the value of the dollar was fixed
at a certain quantity of both gold and silver, with a rate of exchange
between the two metals that had varied between 15 to 1 and 16 to 1.
Since the market value of the two metals often diverged from the
official ratio, one or the other would be minted and the other would
be withdrawn from the market and hoarded. For example, if the
government set the value of 15 ounces of silver at one ounce of gold,
but on the open market one ounce of gold would buy 15.5 ounces of

silver, then silver was officially overvalued. Under these circumstances, silver was minted and used as money while gold, worth more than the official value, went out of circulation. After the inflationary period of the Civil War, there were intense disputes between those who wanted to return to sound money and those who argued that inflating the money supply would produce prosperity. The advocates of inflation were divided between those who called for unbacked paper—fiat money—and those who favored minting and circulating more silver. The sound money party prevailed in 1873 with the Coinage Act, which ended bimetallism, but the conflict was far from over. The silverites responded with the Bland-Allison Act in 1878 and the Sherman Silver Purchase Act in 1890. Back in office with a Democratic Congress, Cleveland was determined to restore gold-standard stability. Supporters urged him to call a special session of Congress to repeal the Sherman Silver Purchase Act and return to the gold standard, but his tactic was to wait until the public came to see the problems more clearly. Before that could happen, however, Cleveland faced two simultaneous crises—cancer and the worst economic depression in American history up to that point.

On May 5, as the economy was teetering on the precipice, Cleveland noticed a spot in the roof of his mouth that was tender and swollen. For several weeks, he dismissed it as caused by a bad tooth, but as the pain increased, he had it checked by Dr. R. M. O'Reilly, the White House physician. He diagnosed the site, about the size of a quarter, as cancerous. Dr. William Welch of Johns Hopkins University also examined the biopsied tissue and confirmed O'Reilly's diagnosis. Further confirmation came from Dr. Joseph D. Bryant, a New York surgeon and a good friend of Cleveland's, who advised an immediate operation. Cleveland agreed but insisted on secrecy lest fear about the president's condition exacerbate the economic and political crisis. Bryant assembled a distinguished medical team for the operation, which would take place on the *Oneida*, a yacht owned by Cleveland's friend Elias Benedict.

On June 30, the president left Washington by train for New York City, where he boarded the *Oneida*, which then set sail for Long Island Sound. The surgery took place the next day. The malignancy and surrounding tissue were removed in a one-hour procedure that entailed cutting out the upper left jaw and removing two teeth. Bleeding was minimal, and there were no post-operative complications. Great care had been taken by the surgical team to sterilize the area to be operated upon as well as the medical personnel themselves and the instruments used. Cleveland, a robust man, was up and about the next day. Since the surgery was confined to his mouth, there were no external signs that anything had taken place. A vulcanized rubber prosthesis filled the gap left in his upper jaw, and his appearance was unchanged. With the exception of Dr. Bryant, the other members of the surgical team were dropped off at Sag Harbor on Long Island, and the *Oneida* sailed on for Cape Cod, arriving on July 5 at Gray Gables, where Cleveland was met by his relieved wife, who had been waiting for him there.

Later in July, Dr. Bryant conducted a follow-up procedure, also on the *Oneida*, to make certain that the healing was going well. Some more tissue was removed, the site cauterized, and the Clevelands assured that the prognosis was good. Despite press suspicions about the president's being incommunicado at sea for several days, the whole matter remained a secret until 1917, when one of the physicians, Dr. William W. Keen, a prominent Philadelphia surgeon, wrote about it in the *Saturday Evening Post*. At that time, other confirming recollections came forth. But in 1893, the security screen was not penetrated and Cleveland recovered rapidly.

The president's personal recovery was in fact for more rapid than the economy's. In April, the Pennsylvania Steel Company, a mid-sized operation, went under, compounding the markets' fears that the monetary policy of recent years had devalued the currency. Declining public confidence fueled the redemption of U.S. currency for gold, and the government's gold reserves fell below $100 million, a level considered essential to maintain. On May 3, the stock market was hit by sell-off fever. The next day, one of the most important U.S. corporations, National Cordage, failed. The Panic of 1893 was underway.[6]

Cleveland was convinced that repealing the Sherman Silver Purchase Act and restoring the gold standard were crucial for addressing the crisis. As he later explained in a letter to Governor William J. Northen of Georgia:

> I want a currency that is stable and safe in the hands of our people. I will not knowingly be implicated in a condition that will justly make me in the least degree answerable to any laborer or farmer in the United States for a shrinkage in the purchasing power he has received for a full dollar's worth of work, or for a good dollar's worth of the product of his toil. I not only want our currency to be of such a character that all kinds of dollars will be of equal purchasing power at home, but I want it to be of such a character as will demonstrate abroad our wisdom and good faith, thus placing us upon a firm foundation and credit among

the nations of the earth. I want our financial conditions and
the laws relating to our currency safe and reassuring, that
those who have money will spend and invest it in business
and new enterprises instead of hoarding it. You cannot cure
fright by calling it foolish and unreasonable, and you cannot prevent the frightened man from hoarding his money.
I want good, sound and stable money and a condition of
confidence that will keep it in use.[7]

Cleveland was willing to have silver coins in circulation, but their role
would be subsidiary to that of gold.

The president called Congress into a special session in August for
the purpose of repealing the Sherman Silver Purchase Act. In the
House, which took up the measure first, the issue aroused intense
emotions. William Jennings Bryan, only thirty-three years old and just
beginning his astonishingly swift rise, harangued the body for three
hours. He depicted the debate as a contest between working Americans, "an unnumbered throng, those who gave to the Democratic
party a name and for whom it has assumed to speak," and "the cor-
porate interests of the United States, the moneyed interests, aggregated
wealth and capital, imperious, arrogant, compassionless."[8] It was "a
riveting performance," writes his biographer, "and a blatantly dema-
gogic one."[9]

The power of Bryan's rhetoric would propel him three years later
to the Democratic presidential nomination, but his time had not yet
come in the special session of 1893. Representative William Bourke
Cockran of New York proved more persuasive, effectively articulating
the gold-standard position and explaining the pernicious effects of
abandoning it.[10] Cockran, who had left Ireland for the United States
at seventeen years of age, quoted Adam Smith and John Stuart Mill

from memory. A fellow congressman later wrote, "He showed the learning of a philosopher rather than a pedant and added to it the manner of a gentleman."[11] On August 28, the House voted 239 to 108 to repeal the Sherman Silver Purchase Act.

The debate moved to the Senate, where the sound-money leadership was less impressive.[12] The fight was bitter and prolonged, extending for over two months beyond the date of the House vote. The silverite contingent even resorted to filibustering. By October, the Democrats were weakening in their support of Cleveland's position. Thirty-seven of the forty-four Senate Democrats proposed to Daniel Voorhees, the chairman of the Finance Committee and a leading proponent of repeal, that a compromise be arranged. There was growing pressure for Cleveland to accept "half a loaf." The president vehemently opposed a compromise, banging his fist on the table in a cabinet meeting as he swore that he would not back down. Once Cleveland had determined what was right, neither blandishments nor threats would sway him. His determination stiffened the spines of his wavering congressional allies and discouraged his opponents. On October 30, the Senate voted 48 to 37 for repeal. The return to the gold standard restored both domestic and foreign confidence in the dollar, and by the end of 1893 the worst of the panic was over.[13]

The depression had built up a head of steam, however, and it persisted through the rest of Cleveland's administration. Even though monetary policy had been corrected, there was no instantaneous reversal of the economic downturn, and the rise of the Democratic Party's left wing cost the administration any chance to control the course of events. The advocates of more government control and monetary inflation were more effective than Cleveland at persuading the public. Evaluations of Cleveland's handling of the depression vary according to historians' economic philosophies. In his 1996 history of the Republican Party, Robert Allen Rutland faults him for not pursuing aggressive policies of government intervention and inflation: "Cleveland's philosophy of government prevented him from becoming an activist, ready to use governmental resources to combat the agonizing depression that threw thousands out of work each week."[14]

Bryan's star was rising. In January 1894, Congress passed a bill to increase the coinage of silver. Cleveland vetoed it, citing the danger of inflation. He had staved off the silverite threat but had not eliminated it. How quickly things can change in politics! Through the power of the presidency and his strength of will, Cleveland could still block the populist agenda, but his positive achievements would be few.

Monetary problems continued through 1894 in spite of the repeal of the silver act. The flight of gold from the United States continued as foreign investors still worried about cheap money pressure and sold off their U.S. securities. By the end of 1893, the government's gold reserves had fallen to $60 million. Cleveland and Secretary of the Treasury Carlisle succeeded in selling bonds that brought the gold reserve back to $107 million in January. By November 1894, though, the reserve was down by $46 million. Another bond issue restored the situation only temporarily. By the end of the year, gold reserves fell again as Europeans continued to sell off their American investments. Cleveland remained firm, insisting that government obligations be paid in gold, to the consternation of the growing ranks of cheap-money men, who argued that inflating the money supply by pumping in more silver would solve the problem. Congress blocked any further bond issues and the drain continued.

Cleveland now had to turn to private bankers, especially the financial and industrial giant J. P. Morgan.[15] In February, Morgan went to the White House with Robert Bacon, a key executive in his empire, and Francis Lynde Stetson, who was Morgan's attorney and Cleveland's friend. Upstairs in the White House library, they met with Cleveland, Carlisle, Attorney General Olney, Secretary of War Lamont,[16] and August Belmont Jr., a prominent banker who also represented the English house of Rothschild in the United States.[17]

Morgan, genuinely concerned about the economic health of the country and seeing an opportunity to profit personally, agreed to form and head a syndicate which would sell 3.5 million ounces of gold coin to the government at $17.80 per ounce, receiving $62.3 million in bonds. Gold at the time was selling at $18.60 per ounce, so the government received $65.1 million in gold in return for $62.3 million in bonds. The bonds matured in thirty years, paid 4 percent interest, and could be redeemed in either gold or silver coin, the decision being in the hands of the government.[18]

By June 1895, the gold reserve was back over $100 million. To the credit of Morgan and the others in the syndicate, the plan had worked: gold began flowing back into the United States, and the dollar stabilized. The syndicate sold the bonds they had purchased at a reasonable profit. The Americans involved in the operation cleared just under 5 percent, hardly excessive considering the critical circumstances.[19] The Left, quite predictably, assailed Cleveland and the syndicate for profiteering. In spite of assaults on him and his policies, he remained firm in his support of the gold standard, and he continued to have enough support from likeminded members of Congress to preserve his vetoes. Cleveland's strength in the Democratic Party continued to erode, and nervousness about the economy continued, hampering recovery until after the election of a new administration.

But the American economy eventually righted itself without government stimulus programs.

From the end of the Civil War in 1865 until the Panic of 1893, wages rose steadily, almost doubling at a time when prices were relatively stable. There were important technological advances, and business flourished. Still, there were those who deplored the imperfections of the free market and looked to a future golden age without private property. The spectacular success of Edward Bellamy's 1888 utopian novel, *Looking Backward*—a depiction of future socialist felicity that sold two hundred thousand copies—revealed the extent of economic discontent and inspired a network of "Nationalist Clubs" dedicated to making Bellamy's vision a reality. Still, American society, whatever its shortcomings and challenges, was not ripe for the socialist transformation of which the Bellamyites dreamed, and the Nationalist Clubs had vanished by the mid-1890s.

An extreme reaction to Cleveland was mounted by Jacob Coxey of Ohio, a wealthy farmer and rancher, and came to be called "Coxey's Army." A committed Populist Party man, Coxey called for a massive public works program, primarily the building of roads, to be paid for by printing $500 million in paper money that could not be redeemed in gold or silver. On March 25, 1894, Coxey and a hundred-man entourage that he grandiloquently called the "Army of the Commonwealth of Christ" sallied forth from Massillon, Ohio. By the time they arrived in Washington on May 1, their ranks had swelled to five hundred. But here the movement fizzled. Coxey and a number of his followers were arrested for trespassing on the grounds of the Capitol and the protest fell apart. After paying fines and spending a short time in jail, the members of the "Army" went home. Anyone who studies Coxey's proposals, which seemed impossibly eccentric in 1894, will notice that they bear a striking resemblance to Franklin

Roosevelt's New Deal. The long-lived Coxey himself hung around on the fringes of American politics for several more decades. He was nominee of the Farmer Labor Party in the presidential election of 1932, the year Franklin Roosevelt won his first term and the New Deal began.

1894 also saw the passage of the Wilson-Gorman Tariff Act, an abortive attempt by the Democrats to fulfill their promise to lower tariffs. The House bill lowered rates substantially—to zero, in fact, on wool, coal, lumber, and iron ore. To pay for the anticipated loss of revenue, the bill established the first peacetime income tax in American history. The rate was to be 2 percent on incomes over $4,000, an exaction that would have affected 10 percent of the country's households. Cleveland did not like the idea of an income tax but was persuaded that it was small enough for him to accept in return for the lower tariff rates. He failed to recognize that an income tax was the necessary condition for the growth of government to a previously unimaginable size. The House passed the measure 204 to 140.

In the Senate, however, the bill's co-sponsor Arthur P. Gorman of Maryland managed to knock out most of the lower tariff rates with a barrage of amendments. Cleveland responded with a blistering rebuke that antagonized his opponents and stiffened their resolve. The Senate version passed 39 to 34, with a dozen senators abstaining. Reconciliation resulted in a slight lowering of the McKinley rates. The president had lost this battle. He let the emasculated final version of the bill sit on his desk unsigned and become law after the prescribed lapse of ten days.

The depression that began in 1893 proved to be the worst one the country had yet experienced. The 1894 strike by railroad workers against the Pullman Palace Car Company was emblematic of the souring of labor relations around the country. George Pullman, the company's founder, required employees to live in the company town outside Chicago. On the surface, it was an attractive, desirable location for the workers. There was, though, a darker side. Rents were high, and the residents had to shop in company stores, where prices were higher than in outside stores. As the depression deepened, the Pullman Company reduced wages by an average of 25 percent, but there was no corresponding reduction in rents or the prices in its stores. When a committee of workers called for a reduction in rents and prices if wages could not be raised, they were turned down, three were fired, and the strike began. Then Eugene V. Debs arrived.

Born in Indiana in 1855, Debs went to work at age fourteen, initially in railroad shops, later as a locomotive fireman. Rising quickly in the union movement, he became national secretary and treasurer of the Brotherhood of Locomotive Firemen in 1880 and president of the American Railway Union in 1893. Along the way, he also served short stints as Terre Haute city clerk and as an Indiana state legislator. Debs supported organizing workers by industry, as the American Railway Union did, rather than by individual crafts, the approach favored by Samuel Gompers and the American Federation of Labor.

In 1894, Debs and his organization were prepared to enter the lists in support of the Pullman workers. Earlier that year, the American Railway Union had flexed its muscles, successfully striking James J. Hill's Great Northern Railroad for higher wages.[20]

Debs was reluctant at first to take on the Pullman Company directly, believing that the Pullman workers were too self-contained, not tied enough economically and socially to the larger labor context. The strike continued into June as a local event. The workers and management stayed firm, far apart in their positions. When the American Railway Union held its first annual convention in Chicago on the twelfth of that month, Debs lobbied hard for indirect support such as money and supplies. The rank and file spurned his moderate position and voted for a national boycott of Pullman sleeping cars; they would not operate any trains with these cars.[21] The strike now became national.

In the wake of the American Railway Union's success against the Great Northern, the railroad companies had joined forces. Fired strikers were not difficult to replace in a depression. The two sides dug in for a long and hard fight.

Attorney General Richard Olney, never one to shrink from a good scrap when convinced he was on the right side, was determined to maintain order and to prevent the economy from being hurt by a prolonged disruption of the railroads, the primary means by which goods moved throughout the country. A federal court issued an injunction on July 2 against union activity which would interfere with mail service and with interstate commerce.

Now that his organization had taken its stand, Debs staunchly supported the workers, although he opposed violence and interference with the mail. But violence ensued. At Blue Island, Illinois, near Chicago, a mob of workers attacked a federal marshal and a contingent of deputies. When the marshal reported that his force was inadequate to preserve order without reinforcements, Cleveland ordered troops into Chicago under General Nelson Miles, a veteran of the Civil War and the Indian wars, who commanded the western department. A mob attacked the soldiers, and Cleveland declared martial law in Chicago. Governor John Peter Altgeld, strongly pro-labor, had regarded sending in federal troops as an overreaction and believed that the state militia could do the job.

Many workers resented Cleveland's response to the labor action; tensions escalated. Debs called for a general strike if the Pullman Company would not make concessions, especially rehiring the strikers. Samuel Gompers and the American Federation of Labor, however, refused to support a general strike, and Debs's threat came to nothing.[22] The English-born Gompers favored a more moderate approach to improve the condition of workers and was convinced that management and labor could work together.

Violence flared in early July. Workers seized a mail train, shots were fired, and an engineer was killed. The army took steps pursuant to the declaration of martial law to suppress the disruption of the railroads. The American Railway Union found that it now had little public support. Facing a resolute government and limited support, even from organized labor, the union gave in. Debs was convicted in December of violating the injunction and sentenced to six months in prison. During his incarceration, he studied the writings of Karl Marx, although he never became an advocate of violent revolution. A democratic socialist, he later ran for president five times.

In January 1895, Debs and his fellow defendants applied to the United States Supreme Court for a writ of habeas corpus on the grounds that there was no evidence of their having disobeyed the injunction and that the lower court had exceeded its power and jurisdiction in ordering their imprisonment. On May 27, the Supreme Court ruled unanimously against Debs and the others. Justice David Brewer wrote for the majority that the defendants had violated the injunction and that their conviction and incarceration were legitimate.

Cleveland's firm stand for order went over well with most Americans, although some resented him as a heavy-handed enemy of labor. Attorney General Olney, a strong-willed and capable man, fully supported the administration's handling of the Pullman strike, and Alyn Brodsky suggests that he was in fact in the lead during this episode.[23] While Cleveland respected Olney and listened to him (as he did the other members of his cabinet), there was no question that the president was in charge, that he set the tone for the administration.

Though Cleveland's handling of the Pullman strike was popular, 1894 was a bad year for him. As the depression continued, the left wing of the Democratic Party became increasingly assertive. Governor Ben Tillman of South Carolina, who was elected to the U.S. Senate that year, attacked the president in a particularly colorful speech that captured the intensity of the Populists' frustration:

> When Judas betrayed Christ, his heart was not blacker than this scoundrel Cleveland, in deceiving the Democracy. He is an old bag of beef and I am going to Washington with a pitchfork and prod him in his old fat ribs.[24]

Governor Altgeld of Illinois invoked the same biblical comparison to express his opprobrium. Praising Cleveland on Jefferson's birthday, he declared, was like "sing[ing] a Te Deum to Judas Iscariot on a Christmas morning."[25]

During his second presidential term, Cleveland again filled two vacancies on the Supreme Court. The first, Edward D. White of Louisiana, had served briefly in the Confederate army as a teenager.

After the war, he was a judge in his home state and was a member of the U.S. Senate when nominated as an associate justice in 1894. In 1910, President William Howard Taft elevated him to chief justice upon the death of Melville Fuller. Cleveland's other appointment was Rufus W. Peckham of New York, also a conservative who had served as a judge in his home state. He was not the president's first choice, but he was supported by the Republican-controlled Senate.

The Supreme Court handed down three especially consequential rulings during Cleveland's second term. The first was *United States v. E. C. Knight Co.* In 1892, the American Sugar Refining Company had gained control of several companies, including E. C. Knight, which gave it control of 98 percent of the sugar-refining business in the country. Cleveland considered this a violation of the Sherman Antitrust Act and directed Attorney General Olney to bring a lawsuit against the company. The case made its way to the Supreme Court, which in January 1895 ruled in favor of the company in an 8 to 1 decision. Chief Justice Fuller's opinion held that while commerce is subject to the jurisdiction of the federal government, manufacturing monopolies are not; they come under the purview of the states. Since the refineries were engaged in manufacturing but not interstate commerce, they were not subject to the Sherman Antitrust Act. By the late 1930s, the Court would take a more expansive view of the powers which could be exercised by the United States government.

In April 1895, the court struck down the income tax imposed by the Wilson-Gorman Tariff Act. The 5 to 4 decision in *Pollock v. Farmers' Loan and Trust Company* held that the tax violated Article I, Section 9, of the Constitution, which provides, "No Capitation or other direct, Tax shall be laid, unless in Proportion to the Census or Enumeration herein before directed to be taken." Since the income tax was imposed on individuals irrespective of the state in which they lived, the majority ruled that it violated the Constitution. Cleveland's appointee Melville Fuller voted with the majority in *Pollock* while Edward White dissented.

Support for a tax on personal income, though, was far from dead. The British had imposed an income tax in 1799 to finance the war against France, later repealed it, and reinstated it in the 1880s. To fund the Civil War, the federal government had imposed a tax of 3 percent on incomes over $600. Later in the war, the rate was raised and made progressive. By 1864, the top rate was 10 percent on incomes over $10,000, a high income in those days. The tax had lapsed in 1872, and though it was no longer on the books, it was declared unconstitutional in 1881.[26] But proponents of the income tax persisted, and the narrowness of the ruling in *Pollock* encouraged them. The Sixteenth Amendment to the Constitution was ratified in 1913, providing: "The Congress shall have power to lay and collect taxes on incomes, from whatever source derived, without apportionment among the several States, and without regard to any census or enumeration."

For good or ill, the way was now open for a substantial increase in the power of government.

The third landmark decision delivered during Cleveland's second term, *Plessy v. Ferguson*, is one of the most notorious in the history of the Supreme Court. A Louisiana statute provided: "All railroad companies carrying passengers in their coaches in this State, shall provide equal but separate accommodations for the white, and colored, races."[27] Homer Adolph Plessy, a black man, refused to leave a seat that was reserved for white people. He was arrested and tried for violation of the law. If found guilty, Plessy faced the possibility of a $25 fine or up to twenty days in jail. In his defense, he charged that the law violated the equal protection clause of the Fourteenth Amendment.[28] The case ended up before the Supreme Court for the last word.

Cleveland's racial views were moderate for his time. Though he was favorably impressed by Frederick Douglass, he was not optimistic about the prospects for rapid progress by Americans of African ancestry. He believed they were entitled to the rights of citizenship under the U.S. Constitution but that the Louisiana law under which Plessy had been convicted was a state matter. Cleveland considered black Americans below white Americans in terms of culture, but did not label them as inherently inferior.

On May 8, 1896, the Supreme Court ruled 7 to 1 against Plessy. In the majority opinion, Justice Henry Billings held that the United States Constitution does not mandate "social, as distinguished from political equality."

> Laws permitting, and even requiring, [the races'] separation in places where they are liable to be brought into contact do not necessarily imply the inferiority of either race to the other, and have been generally, if not universally, recognized as within the competency of the state legislatures in the exercise of their police power.[29]

The court concluded that the Louisiana law separating the races in railroad cars was not unreasonable as it did not imply the inferiority of one race to the other:

> We consider the underlying fallacy of the plaintiff's argument to consist in the assumption that the enforced separation of the two races stamps the colored race with a badge of inferiority. If this be so, it is not by reason of anything found in the fact, but solely because the colored race chooses to put that construction on it.[30]

The lone dissenter in *Plessy v. Ferguson* was John Marshall Harlan, a onetime slave owner, who insisted that the Constitution does not permit the law to differentiate between citizens on the basis of race:

> We boast of the freedom enjoyed by our people above all other peoples. But it is difficult to reconcile that boast with a state of law which, practically, puts the brand of servitude and degradation upon a large class of our fellow citizens— our equals before the law. The thin disguise of "equal" accommodations for passengers in railroad coaches will not mislead any one, nor atone for the wrong this day done.[31]

Plessy v. Ferguson's separate-but-equal standard remained in place until 1954, when the Supreme Court overturned it unanimously in *Brown v. Board of Education.*

These three decisions rank among the most influential in our history. To this day, the United States is working to clarify the relationship between the power of the government to regulate the activities of individuals and corporations on the one hand and the freedom of the private sector on the other. Every generation must deal with this issue. Cleveland understood this, and by and large, he achieved the balance.

The Democratic Party was showing signs of being pulled apart, with conservatives moving toward the Republicans and the left-wing activists toward the Populist Party. The Democrats suffered a sharp reversal in the 1894 midterm elections, losing control of both houses of Congress. The Senate went from forty-four Democrats, thirty-nine Republicans, three others, and three vacancies to forty-four Republicans, thirty-nine Democrats, and five others. The change in the House of Representatives was more dramatic—from 220 Democrats, 126 Republicans, and eight others to 246 Republicans, 104 Democrats, and seven others.[32]

William Jennings Bryan prevented the disintegration of the Democratic Party two years later by pulling it to the left and undercutting the Populists. Despite the party's survival, however, it took another two decades and a split among the Republicans for it to fully recover.

The stress of bad economic times led some to blame their woes on Cleveland, even to the extent of sending him threatening letters. Frances became so concerned about the safety of her family that she urged her husband to increase the security at the Executive Mansion. The security detail was increased from two men to twenty-seven.[33]

Cleveland's second term presented him with more foreign policy challenges than his first. An opponent of imperialism, he was nevertheless no pacifist. He had no illusions about the intentions of other countries, and he did not shrink from protecting American interests. The expansion of European influence in the Americas and the eastern Pacific, Cleveland believed, was inimical to American interests and unjust to the inhabitants of those regions. He had demonstrated his determination in the Samoan crisis of his first term. As his second term began in 1893, he faced three potentially explosive situations: the question of Hawaii's future, the border squabble between Venezuela and British Guiana, and the Cuban rebellion against Spain.

The protection of America's far-flung commercial and political interests required a large and effective navy, and there was bipartisan support for its modernization and growth, which had begun during the Arthur administration. By the end of the Civil War, the American fleet was second only to the Royal Navy. Thereafter, interest in maintaining strong armed forces dropped rapidly, and by 1870 the U.S. Navy ranked twelfth in the world and was technologically backward.

Perhaps the most important figure in the history of America's naval expansion was Alfred Thayer Mahan, whose writings made the historical and strategic case for naval power. Born in 1840, he graduated from the United States Naval Academy and served in combat during the Civil War. Although he had a distinguished career as a naval officer, Mahan's strengths lay more in scholarship and strategic thought than in commanding ships. In 1884, he joined the faculty of the new Naval War College in Newport, Rhode Island, and in 1886 began a three-year term as its president. In 1890, he published his masterpiece, *The Influence of Sea Power Upon History, 1660–1783*; its impact was quick and deep. The book was widely read in naval circles around the world, especially in Great Britain and in Germany. Mahan argued that control of the seas was essential for the development and prosperity of great powers. His ideas attracted influential supporters, such as Theodore Roosevelt, whose *The Naval War of 1812* had already drawn attention to the importance of naval power, and Cleveland's secretary of the navy, Hilary Herbert. During Roosevelt's own presidency, the U.S. Navy became the third-largest in the world, and during World War II it surpassed even the storied British fleet.

The globe in Cleveland's day was dominated by the great European empires. The British Empire was at its height in the late nineteenth century. Germany, recently united, had come late to the imperial contest and was grabbing what was still available, taking over large pieces of Africa as well as the Marshall Islands, part of New Guinea, and part of Samoa in the Pacific. France had an extensive overseas empire, including in the Pacific, but was focused primarily on a rematch with Germany in Europe after losing the Franco-Prussian War of 1870–1871. In the last decade of the century, Japan was well on its way to becoming a major power and was probing into Hawaii, where many of its subjects had moved. There were still those who viewed the British as the greatest threat to America, but concern about the strength and expansion of Germany and Japan was growing.

Hawaii's strategic location, from which power could be projected throughout the eastern and central Pacific, made it a focus of imperial ambitions. Polynesian explorers had reached the islands two thousand years earlier, but Europeans knew nothing of them until Captain James Cook of Great Britain arrived in 1778. Lacking natural resistance, the native Hawaiians were decimated by European diseases such as smallpox and measles. The population of the islands fell from an estimated 300,000 when the Europeans arrived to 108,000 in 1836 and 73,000 in 1853. The depopulation opened opportunities for immigrants from the United States, China, Japan, and Europe.

Kamehameha, a chief on the island of Hawaii, launched a bloody war in 1782 for control of that island. By 1792 he had won, and in 1795 he set up himself as King Kamehameha I, having conquered most of the island chain. Unification was complete by 1810 and the kingdom well established. The king died in 1819 and was succeeded by his son Kamehameha II, who ended the establishment of the old Hawaiian religion, permitting individuals to choose freely, and Christian missionaries succeeded in bringing the king himself into the fold.[34]

Kamehameha II died in 1824 and was succeeded by his brother, Kamehameha III, under whom Christianity became the official faith of the realm. Hawaii became a constitutional monarchy with a written constitution in 1840. The legislative branch was comprised of a council of chiefs and an elected house of representatives. The United States granted diplomatic recognition to the new regime in 1842, and the British and the French soon followed.[35]

Diplomatic recognition, however, was not a guarantee of Hawaiian independence. In 1843, a group of Englishmen, with connivance of the commander of a Royal Navy frigate then in Honolulu harbor, mounted a coup; the Hawaiian flag was lowered and the Union Jack raised. The British government, though, countermanded this action and restored the Hawaiian government. Britain had bigger imperial fish to fry in India and Africa; Hawaii was not worth the diplomatic cost that such a seizure would entail. The Hawaiians were reminded again of their vulnerability during this golden age of European expansion. Careful diplomacy would be necessary to play different potential occupiers against one another while securing the assistance of foreigners in developing the economy. The Hawaiians played this game successfully for several decades, though American influence grew progressively stronger.

In 1874, David Kalakaua ascended the throne at the age of thirty-seven. Physically imposing, he was a man of intelligence and charm. He was fascinated with the military and trained with and served as an officer in Hawaii's small force. He studied American law, traveled extensively in the West, and dreamed of uniting Polynesians into one Pacific realm under his own rule. But Kalakaua degenerated into a pleasure-seeking, corrupt ruler, and his expansive dreams could not overcome the reality that Hawaii was a strategically located chain of islands with a small population and weak armed forces confronted by dynamic western countries confidently spreading to the far corners of the earth. He eventually lost control of his realm to ambitious Americans who had moved to the islands. A new constitution in 1887 substantially reduced the power of the monarchy. That same year, the United States was granted rights to Pearl Harbor.[36]

Kalakaua died in 1891 and was succeeded by his sister, Liliuokalani. The last Hawaiian monarch, she tried to restore the kingdom's independence with a new constitution that would increase her power and reduce that of outsiders. The 1887 constitution permitted citizens of foreign countries to vote in Hawaiian elections as long as they met residency requirements. In January 1893, Liliuokalani attempted to promulgate the new constitution without the support of the legislature, which had voted it down. Her cabinet, mindful of the political winds, refused to support her.[37] At this point, Hawaiian citizens of American background (about two thousand in number) and American business interests in the islands organized a provisional government with the covert support of John Stevens, the American minister. Marines and sailors from the USS *Boston* landed in Honolulu, ostensibly to protect American lives and property but in fact to deter opposition to the impending overthrow of Liliuokalani. Although there were Hawaiians prepared to fight,[38] and the royalist troops outnumbered those of the provisional government and the Americans from the *Boston*, there was little appetite for fighting the inevitable. Liliuokalani yielded to the superior American power, but she refused to abdicate, calling for American justice.

Benjamin Harrison had favored annexation of Hawaii as long as it could be presented as representing the will of the people there. But Cleveland, suspicious of the circumstances surrounding the change in government, withdrew the annexation treaty from Senate consideration and appointed a special commissioner to investigate. When the report confirmed Cleveland's suspicion that American power had been misused, he ruled out annexation and called for the reinstatement of Liliuokalani as queen.

The new government in Hawaii was headed by Sanford Dole, the Hawaiian-born son of American missionaries. After completing his studies in the United States, Dole had returned to the islands as a lawyer, eventually serving in the legislature and as a justice of the Hawaiian supreme court. In the face of Cleveland's opposition to annexation, Dole organized the Republic of Hawaii in 1894 and was elected president. The next year, Liliuokalani formally abdicated and retired to her Honolulu mansion, where she lived until her death in 1917.[39] Hawaii continued as an independent republic until the next administration, that of William McKinley, took office and American expansion was back in vogue. Hawaii was annexed in 1898, a decision Cleveland opposed.

On January 24 of that year, he issued a statement to the Associated Press reminding readers that he had blocked annexation in 1893:

> I regarded, and still regard, the proposed annexation of these islands as not only opposed to our national policy, but as a perversion of our national mission. The mission of our nation is to build up and make a greater country out of what we have, instead of annexing islands.[40]

Cleveland, in his principled stand, ignored the *Realpolitik* of the day. The question was not whether Hawaii would remain independent or become an American possession but whether Hawaii would become American or be absorbed by Britain or Germany.

The border between Venezuela and British Guiana had been in dispute for much of the nineteenth century. In 1894, lobbying by

Venezuela in the United States struck a responsive chord with many Americans. The Monroe Doctrine was well established, and most Americans firmly opposed expanded European influence in their hemisphere. Venezuela was seen as the underdog, and anti-British feeling still ran strong among many Americans. Apart from moral and political considerations, there was concern for American trade.

Cleveland was hardening the U.S. stance against what he saw as British heavy-handedness when Secretary of State Walter Q. Gresham died. Impressed with Attorney General Richard Olney's assertiveness and strong convictions, Cleveland appointed him Gresham's successor. Olney would brook no expansion of European power in the Americas. The United States sought no empire, but Olney believed it should exercise a tutelary role in the Western Hemisphere that would diminish European influence. American economic interests would benefit from such a policy, to be sure, but the administration had genuine hopes for the development of order, justice, and freedom in Latin America. Many years of American involvement in the region lay ahead, and many Latin Americans would come to resent Yankee paternalism.

Olney sent a strong message to the British asserting that the Western Hemisphere was the United States' sphere of influence. Formulating what came to be known as the "Olney Corollary" to the Monroe Doctrine, also known as the "Olney Interpretation," he declared that the United States would mediate border disputes in its own hemisphere, barring outside countries from asserting power in the Americas. The British sat on Olney's message for a few months, then rejected the notion that the dispute concerned the United States. The president then reaffirmed the Monroe Doctrine and announced that the U.S. would not tolerate its violation: "The Monroe [D]octrine finds its recognition in those principles of international law which are based upon the theory that every nation shall have its rights protected and its just claims enforced."[41]

Concluding his message, he proclaimed,

> I am, nevertheless, firm in my conviction that while it is a grievous thing to contemplate the two great English-speaking peoples of the world as being otherwise than friendly competitors in the onward march of civilization and strenuous and worthy rivals in all the arts of peace, there is no calamity which a great nation can invite which equals that which follows a supine submission to wrong and injustice and the consequent loss of national self-respect and honor, beneath which are shielded and defended a people's safety and greatness.[42]

While support for war with Britain increased, some Americans were alarmed by the president's bellicose stand and the preparations for conflict. Cleveland castigated these critics for their timidity or for being primarily concerned with the potential dangers to their personal financial positions. These people, he wrote, would support principles like the Monroe Doctrine as long as said principles did not interfere with their private lives.[43] Cleveland was convinced that his position enhanced the country's international reputation and impressed the British. Most of the country, he believed, was with him.[44]

In the face of American resolve, the British indicated a willingness to talk, and back-channel negotiations began. The two countries reached a peaceful resolution in 1899, after Cleveland had left office. The British were concerned with bigger problems than the Venezuelan border dispute. Germany was a growing naval, military, and industrial threat. Russia was expanding its empire in Europe and in the Far East as well as beginning to reach southward toward India. Expansion in South America was desirable, but not worth a clash with the United States, which might revive American interest in Canada. Common sense prevailed, and an international tribunal came up with a compromise which avoided a conflict.

Cuba was another place with the potential to draw the United States into international conflict. Christopher Columbus had claimed the island for Spain in 1492. The Spanish settled in 1511, defeating and enslaving the inhabitants, a fate which few survived. African slaves were brought in, providing the labor for the increasingly successful sugar plantations. Through the eighteenth and nineteenth centuries, sugar production grew until 1860, when almost one-third of the world supply came from Cuba.

Alarmed by a major slave uprising that broke out in 1812, most white settlers preferred Spanish rule to the independence movement sweeping through the Spanish Americas. By the middle part of the century, some Cubans, especially slave owners, favored joining the United States, a sentiment reciprocated by pro-slavery Americans concerned with the faster population and economic growth by the anti-slavery North, but also by others who wanted to see an end to the harsh Spanish occupation. Spain rejected three American offers to purchase Cuba.

In 1868, the Ten Years' War began. A movement of poor whites, mulattoes, free blacks, and slaves seeking the establishment of an independent republic and the abolition of slavery, it resulted in some reforms but was followed by another rebellion, the Little War, in 1879 and 1880. The Spanish finally ended slavery in 1886. The Cuban

Revolutionary Party, led by José Martí, revived the cause of independence in 1892, and the war for independence erupted in 1895. Cuban refugees in the United States fanned the flames against Spanish rule.

Cleveland has been accused of having "sympathized with Spain and let them try to subdue the revolt,"[45] but the truth is more complicated. The administration faced a dilemma. Cleveland, along with most Americans, sympathized with the Cubans, but he believed that the continued occupation of the island by a weak Spain was preferable to an independent but disunited Cuba that would be vulnerable to absorption by another European empire. He hoped for a compromise that would give Cuba more autonomy but not full independence.

On June 12, 1895, Cleveland issued a proclamation of American neutrality and ordered the navy and the Revenue Cutter Service (a predecessor of the Coast Guard) to interdict aid from the United States to the Cuban rebels.[46] This policy was unpopular. The Hearst and Pulitzer newspapers were especially successful in whipping up anti-Spanish sentiment.

Secretary of State Olney had come to see the Cuban rebellion as a genuine national movement rather than an uprising by the rabble that would lead to anarchy. He was angered, though, by the destruction of American property in Cuba and by the war fever of the press. He also was alarmed by rumors that Spain, worn down by the struggle, might sell the island, possibly to Germany, a country looking to expand its empire in the Caribbean as well as in the Pacific, in Africa, and in Asia. Olney and Cleveland therefore persisted in the policy of neutrality, setting the administration at odds with public opinion. On April 6, 1896, the House of Representatives passed, by a huge margin, a concurrent resolution authorizing the president to give belligerent rights to the Cuban rebels, a move just short of full recognition. The president also was authorized to intervene, if necessary, to protect

American interests. Cleveland said nothing and the congressional session ended.[47]

The administration offered to mediate the conflict, promising both Spanish sovereignty and Cuban self-rule,[48] something like the dominion status later granted to parts of the British Empire. It was many years too late, however, for such a compromise.

While there were no foreign policy catastrophes to add to Cleveland's woes, neither was there any overwhelming success to burnish his fading image or to distract attention for long from domestic economic problems. Looking back on his presidency, Cleveland offered this evaluation of the difficult period of 1894 to 1895:

> During those years unhappy currency complications compelled executive resort to heroic treatment for the preservation of our nation's financial integrity, and forced upon the administration a constant, unrelenting struggle for sound money; a long and persistent executive effort to accomplish beneficent and satisfactory tariff reform so nearly miscarried as to bring depression and disappointment to the verge of discouragement; and it was at the close of the year 1895 that executive insistence upon the Monroe Doctrine culminated in a situation that gave birth to solemn thoughts of war.[49]

His stance against British expansion in the Venezuelan dispute was popular, but the issue soon faded. Cleveland's standing remained high with the conservative wing of his party, the so-called "Bourbon Democrats," who heartily approved his sound money, limited government, and pro-business policies. This segment, though, was losing ground as the populist wing of the party, which saw business and successful individuals as elements of society that had to be controlled more and taxed more, grew in power. The unwritten tradition of a two-term limit ensured that Cleveland's days as the leader of the Democratic Party would come to an end with the 1896 election. The Bourbon Democrats feared that a shift in the party was coming, but the intensity of the change would astonish them.

CHAPTER 8

TRANSITION

THE REPUBLICANS CONVENED FIRST in 1896, holding their national convention in St. Louis from June 16 through 18. The Speaker of the House, Thomas Reed of Maine, and Senator William Boyd Allison of Iowa had thrown their hats into the presidential ring, but neither could engender much support. The clear front-runner was Governor William McKinley of Ohio, who had been a major during the Civil War and a member of the House of Representatives for fourteen years. He enjoyed the support of the Ohio industrialist and later U.S. senator Mark Hanna, one of the premier "king-makers" in American history. The nomination went to McKinley on the first ballot. Garret Hobart of New Jersey was selected as his running mate.

The Republican Party was dominated by proponents of the gold standard, whose position was strengthened by the recognition that the Democrats were sorely divided over the issue and that this was the time to draw many conservative Democrats to the McKinley-Hobart ticket. McKinley had gravitated to a firmer gold standard position and Hobart definitely favored it.

The Democratic national convention, held in Chicago three weeks later, was considerably more exciting than the Republicans', producing one of the most dramatic changes of course in American political history. Cleveland did not openly endorse a successor at the convention. Since he was not a candidate, he believed that he should not try to influence the convention, but he also recognized that most of the delegates had rejected his conservative stance. Behind the scenes, he favored either Secretary of the Treasury John G. Carlisle, who earlier had served as speaker of the House and as a member of the Senate, or former Massachusetts Governor William Russell. But Cleveland's day had passed, and neither man gained any traction. Conservative Democrats knew that their control of the party was in peril, but the magnitude of their repudiation would come as a tremendous shock. Cleveland was determined to keep the Democratic Party committed to the gold standard, but the situation was rapidly slipping out of his control. Although some states, such as Pennsylvania, Massachusetts, and Michigan, supported a sound-money platform, state after state went for free silver and selected national convention delegates pledged to nominate silverites for president and vice president. As the convention opened, many saw Representative Richard "Silver Dick" Bland of Missouri as the most likely presidential nominee. He was well known as a proponent of the free coinage of silver, but he was relegated to the historical backwaters when a young man from Nebraska galvanized the delegates with an historic speech.

William Jennings Bryan, just thirty-six years old, had served two terms in the House of Representatives, where he demonstrated his oratorical flair, and had lost a bid for the Senate in 1894. He then edited the *Omaha World-Herald* and lectured extensively, primarily on the monetary controversy, achieving national prominence in 1896. A devout Christian and a public policy liberal, Bryan would dominate the Democratic Party for a dozen years and retain a popular following until his death in 1925. Even though party leaders such as Governor John Peter Altgeld of Illinois urged him to bide his time and support Bland for the 1896 nomination, Bryan was determined to grab the brass ring now.

The conservative Democrats vigorously contested the elections for convention leadership positions—temporary chairman, chairman of the resolutions (platform) committee, keynote speaker—but lost each vote. The platform's repudiation of the gold standard amounted to a repudiation of the Cleveland administration. It was an extraordinary about-face for a national party. On July 9, the third day of the convention, the pro-silver and the pro-gold leaders marshaled their forces. Leading off for the silverites was Senator Ben Tillman of South Carolina, known as "Pitchfork Ben" for his saying of Cleveland that "He is an old bag of beef and I am going to Washington with a pitch fork and prod him in his old fat ribs."[1] He managed to antagonize many in the audience with the stridency of his remarks, boasting, for example, of South Carolina as "the home of secession."[2]

Leading off for the gold-standard side was Senator David B. Hill of New York, the former governor and long-time rival of Cleveland. Hill now stood foursquare for the gold standard. Free silver, he said, "smacks of Populism and Communism." He affirmed "I am a Democrat; but not a revolutionist."[3] His address, well presented, excited few delegates. A similar lack of success met Senator William Vilas of

Wisconsin, who had served as postmaster general and secretary of the interior under Cleveland. The last speaker from this side was former Governor William Russell of Massachusetts who had been regarded by some conservatives as a prospective presidential candidate. Now, though, he was frail and his voice weak, and in a matter of days he would be dead at thirty-nine. With the delegates restless and yearning for battle, William Jennings Bryan ascended the stage and electrified the convention with one of the most dramatically successful speeches in American history.

Bryan had a clear voice and the volume to fill halls in those days before electronic amplification. His dramatic flair, wit, and eloquence galvanized audiences. Here, he spoke for the income tax, for workers and farmers, for the "common man." He closed with the ringing challenge:

> Having behind us the producing masses of this nation and the world, supported by the commercial interests, the laboring interests, and the toilers everywhere, we will answer their demand for a gold standard by saying to them: You shall not press down upon the brow of labor this crown of thorns, you shall not crucify mankind upon a cross of gold.[4]

After a brief pause, the hall erupted into support for Bryan. With this speech, about twenty minutes long, he surged from being a mid-level Democratic politician to the front rank of national leaders.

The nomination, however, was not yet his. The party rank and file may have been thrilled by Bryan, but party leaders feared that he was too young and too new to win a national election. Bland led on the first ballot the next day with 235 delegates to Bryan's 137. But enthusiasm for Bryan was seeping upward, affecting these party chieftains. His support increased on the subsequent ballots until he surged past the requisite two-thirds majority on the fifth ballot. The convention then chose Arthur Sewall of Maine as Bryan's running mate, a man who also called for a national income tax and the free coinage of silver. The delegates included a free-silver plank in the party's platform by an overwhelming margin of 628 to 301. In their hour of triumph, the progressives rejected any conciliatory gesture toward the conservatives, an attitude that would cost Bryan dearly in the general election. A dejected Hill wrote to Daniel Lamont, "I am still a Democrat; very still."[5]

After Bryan's nomination, some conservative Democrats tried to persuade Cleveland to run for reelection on a third-party ticket. The president turned them down for the same reasons he had declined to run for the Democratic nomination—adherence to the two-term tradition and his sense that his time had passed. Calling themselves the National Democratic Party, these conservatives held a convention in Indianapolis, nominating Senator John M. Palmer of Illinois for president and former Governor Simon Bolivar Buckner of Kentucky as his running mate. During the Civil War, Palmer, now seventy-nine, had served as a general in the Union army and Buckner, now seventy-three, as a general in the Confederate army. It was an elderly ticket, but it emphasized national unity, moving beyond any residual sectional resentment. Palmer could support the Republican's platform, but he opposed McKinley's high tariff policy. Cleveland encouraged the National Democrats behind the scenes.[6] On September 5, he wrote to Senator William Vilas of Wisconsin, who had been the postmaster general and secretary of the interior during his first term:

> I am delighted with the outcome of the Indianapolis Convention and as a Democrat I feel very grateful to those who have relieved the bad political atmosphere with such a delicious infusion of fresh air. Every Democrat, after reading the platform, ought to thank God that the glorious principles of our party have found defenders who will not permit them to be polluted by impure hands.[7]

The aging warriors Palmer and Buckner demonstrated commendable vigor, and they enjoyed the support of the *New York Times* and of the limited-government, sound-money Democrats. But McKinley also favored limited government and sound money, and the fear of a Bryan victory drove many conservative Democrats to support the Republican ticket. Cleveland did not join them—he disagreed with McKinley on tariffs and was too firmly identified as a Democrat—but he took no part in the campaign and quietly approved of Bryan's loss.

The Populist Party too was dismayed by Bryan's nomination, but for opposite reasons. The Nebraskan was too conservative for them. The Populists had hoped Bryan would join them and lead them to power or at least make them a major party. The Democrats did not adopt the socialist planks of the Populist platform but stole their thunder by calling for the free coinage of silver, the redistribution of wealth through taxes on the rich, and more regulation of the economy. Most Populists, even the future Socialist Party standard bearer Eugene Debs, considered Bryan a major step forward. Others feared that endorsing the Democratic nominee would compromise the purity of the Populist cause.

When the Populists convened in St. Louis on July 22, intense debate broke out between these factions. James Weaver, the 1892 presidential candidate, nominated Bryan, predicting that his election would bring about "a new Pentecost."[8] One delegate borrowed Bryan's own words to oppose his nomination: "We will not crucify the People's Party on the cross of Democracy."[9, 10] Most Populists, however, supported Bryan with varying degrees of enthusiasm. As a token of independence, they nominated Tom Watson of Georgia for vice president while going along with the Democrats' choice of Bryan to head the ticket.

The momentous election of 1896 presented voters with a sharp contrast between the parties. The major party candidates campaigned vigorously but in different ways. For the most part, McKinley addressed delegation after delegation, group after group, from the front porch of his home in Canton, Ohio. Between June 19 and November, 750,000 people flocked to Canton and stood on his lawn to hear him.[11] Bryan, by contrast, constantly was on the move, his peripatetic campaign crossing the country by rail. Sleeping little, he traveled eighteen thousand miles and addressed about five million people. The fear of what Bryan might do as president, however, cost him too many conservative and moderate votes, and the Republican campaign was better organized and better funded. On November 3, McKinley carried twenty-three states with 271 electoral votes, Bryan twenty-two states with 176 electoral votes. McKinley received 7,104,779 popular votes; voting for Bryan on the Democratic line were 6,502,925, while an additional 222,583 cast their ballots for him as the Populist nominee, giving him a total of 6,725,508 votes.

A bitter William Jennings Bryan blamed Cleveland for the result. But Bryan's defeat was a rejection of Bryan, not of Cleveland. The National Democratic slate of Palmer and Buckner won 133,148 votes.

Although Palmer's showing was not impressive, he drew enough votes in Michigan, Indiana, Kentucky, and West Virginia to nudge those states into the McKinley column.[12] Even though some Western silver Republicans voted for Bryan, the division over monetary policy hurt the Democrats more than the Republicans. Many silver Republicans were put off by Bryan's advocacy of low tariffs, and the Republican outreach to gold Democrats was more effective than Democratic overtures to silver Republicans. The number of silver Republicans was limited. There were attempts to start a new party, but they never gained momentum, and after 1900 most of these renegades were back in the Republican fold.

The Democratic Party's move to the left doomed the Populist Party. James Weaver, for example, joined the Democrats, while some of the most fervent Populists, such as Eugene Debs, migrated to the Socialist Party. The Populists and the Socialists ultimately shared the fate of every third party thus far in American history. After a moment of fanfare, they sank into obscurity when one of the major parties cut the ground from under them, and the charismatic leader who sparked their rise returned to a major party.

1896 was a good year for Theodore Roosevelt, who campaigned vigorously for McKinley and the gold standard, comparing Bryan and the silverites to the French revolutionaries. Roosevelt followed Bryan around the key Midwestern states of Illinois, Michigan, and Minnesota, matching the popular appeal and colorful persona of the Democrat. These three states went for McKinley, increasing Roosevelt's stature. In addition to winning the presidency, the Republicans retained control of Congress, which they had captured in 1894. All in all, this was a banner year for them. For the Democrats, the future was considerably less rosy. Although they had carried twenty-two states and 47.7 percent of the popular vote, the party's disarray seriously weakened the prospect of its return to power any time soon.

Cleveland felt repudiated by most of the country, and by his own party in particular. When his old enemy David Hill had proposed a resolution at the national convention praising "the honesty, economy, courage and fidelity of the present Democratic National Administration," it was overwhelmingly rejected, 564 to 357.[13] Despite the sting of rejection, Cleveland was president until March, and he had to soldier on.

Cleveland was as active a chief executive as ever in the period between the election and McKinley's inauguration. The Cuban and Venezuelan crises continued to boil. On December 7, he delivered his last annual message to Congress, reporting that neither side had been able to gain control of Cuba. The Spaniards held Havana and the major population centers, while the rebels were dominant elsewhere, controlling about two-thirds of the island. Cleveland castigated both sides for abuses and observed that conditions were worsening. In spite of the widespread suffering caused in Cuba, the United States, he said, had maintained a strict policy of neutrality and had not trespassed on Spanish sovereignty. His message contained a clear warning to Spain, however, that the U.S. could not remain on the sidelines indefinitely. If Spain did not bring reforms to Cuba, the time could come "in which our obligations to the sovereignty of Spain will be superseded by higher obligations."[14] Cleveland's sense of justice was strong and his patience had limits, but his term was almost over.

In January, Cleveland submitted to the Senate an arbitration treaty with Britain to resolve the Venezuelan crisis. For five years, disputes between the two countries would be submitted to arbitration. The Senate, however, rejected the treaty for a variety of reasons. Cleveland was a lame duck, and Senate Republicans saw no reason not to wait for a Republican president to take up the issue. Some silverites had no use for Britain, which was the primary advocate of the gold standard. Still others opposed the treaty because they wanted a more assertive U.S. foreign policy. Cleveland was neither an isolationist nor a pacifist, but he did not desire an American empire and he did not want a fight with the British.

A few days before leaving office, the "veto president" vetoed an immigration bill. He was not a nativist, but he wanted to ensure that newcomers assimilated into American life.[15] This bill, introduced by Senator Henry Cabot Lodge of Massachusetts, would have banned illiterate immigrants over sixteen years of age. Cleveland considered the restriction too harsh and killed the bill.

On March 4, 1897, a clear and relatively mild day, Grover Cleveland left the presidency, dismayed that his party had rejected principles that he believed were necessary for the health of the country yet convinced that he had done his best to defend them. Even though he had referred to the National Democratic ticket of Palmer and Buckner as "a delicious infusion of fresh air,"[16] he understood that there was no realistic prospect for their victory and that McKinley, whom he considered a man of honor and much soundness, certainly was preferable as president to Bryan. McKinley too had softened his opinion, having come to admire Cleveland's integrity and strength during the past four years. They had a cordial meeting the night before the inauguration. In their conversation, McKinley professed his support for Cleveland's Cuba policy and his intention to continue it,[17] a policy that was soon swept aside by Spain's growing repressiveness in Cuba, the sinking of the *Maine*, and the overwhelming national sentiment for war, especially in Republican ranks. They discussed the necessity of the gold standard, which remained in place well into the twentieth century until President Nixon cut the dollar's last tenuous tie to gold in 1971.

After the inauguration, Cleveland spent two weeks fishing and duck hunting in North Carolina before beginning the last chapter of his life. He was tired, and his once robust constitution was starting to weaken. There would not be another return to the arena, but his interest in events, and even a degree of involvement, would continue in the time that remained to him. He now was ready for a slower pace, more time to enjoy his family, which would continue to grow. Overall, a good final chapter lay ahead for Cleveland and his loved ones.

⸎ CHAPTER 9 ⸎

TWILIGHT

THE LAST ELEVEN YEARS of Cleveland's life were a time of contentment. Out of office, his reputation recovered from its political battering, and he became a revered elder statesman. The Clevelands were drawn to quiet, conservative, academic Princeton, New Jersey, as the place to spend his retirement. Cleveland's father had studied there, and the university was still grounded in the Presbyterian faith, though its Christian character would be considerably diluted under the presidency of Woodrow Wilson, who was still a professor in 1897.

Cleveland purchased Westland, a large home in Princeton that had been built by Robert Stockton, a naval officer who was a key figure in the conquest of California during the Mexican War and later a senator from New Jersey. As at Gray Gables on Cape Cod, Cleveland's creative senses were invigorated at Westland, and he had a two-story wing added to it. The house sat on five acres, ensuring a good degree of privacy.[1]

Cleveland left office just shy of his sixtieth birthday, and he was by no means ready to spend his days in a rocking chair. At first, he looked forward to rest and relaxation, feeling weary after his difficult second term and his political repudiation by so many of his country-men. On most mornings, he arose between seven and eight, ate break-fast, read the newspapers, and walked into town for the mail. He read, planned alterations to Westland, and fished or went on carriage rides with Frances. Dinner was formal, generally with guests. Most evenings were spent at home, playing billiards or cribbage with friends. The arrival of two more children—Richard, born in 1897, and Francis Grover, born in 1903—capped his domestic happiness.

In June 1897, Princeton University awarded Cleveland an honor-ary doctor of laws degree. Now in retirement with no favors that he could bestow, he accepted this honor. During his active political years, he had rejected previous offers so as to avoid any potential conflict of interest.

Cleveland was not wealthy, but he had saved and invested wisely, and his family enjoyed a comfortable standard of living. To supple-ment his income, he wrote magazine articles about his years in office or about current events. He wrote for the *Saturday Evening Post*, *Century*, *Atlantic Monthly*, and *Ladies' Home Journal*. On the lighter side, he published a series of articles on hunting and fishing under the title *Fishing and Shooting Sketches*.

His major work was a book, *Presidential Problems*, based on lectures he delivered at Princeton on four thorny issues that he had confronted as chief executive—"The Independence of the Executive," "The Government in the Chicago Strike of 1894," "The Bond

Issues," and "The Venezuelan Boundary Controversy." Writing with the advantage of historical perspective, Cleveland considered the problem, with which he was intimately acquainted, of a presidential candidate winning the popular vote but losing the electoral vote. An outcome like that of 1888 troubled Cleveland, but he understood that no human system will ever be perfect. "It seems almost ungracious," he wrote, "to find fault with our present method of electing a President when we recall the alternative from which we escaped, through the final action of the convention which framed the Constitution."[2]

Cleveland's Christian understanding of fallen human nature made him well aware of men's proclivity to put themselves and their interests ahead of all other considerations. But his faith in the divine grace and Providence left him with a certain optimism. In the preface to *Presidential Problems*, Cleveland expressed his confidence that, "notwithstanding the overweening desire among our people for personal and selfish reward of effort, there still exists, underneath it all, a sedate and unimpaired interest in the things that illustrate the design, the traditions and the power of our Government...."[3]

Friends and supporters urged Cleveland to write his autobiography. He never did so, and the reason is not clear. He said that future generations could learn certain lessons from his life, but he was concerned that younger people might not be interested in him. He was popular with the students at Princeton, however. His lectures were well attended, and the students celebrated the birth of his last two sons. It could have been that Cleveland was showing the cumulative effects of years under fire, especially in his second term, that his courage and strength did not make him immune to the feeling that his time had passed. Perhaps he never wrote an autobiography because he believed that his record spoke for itself.

In October 1901, Cleveland was selected to serve as a trustee of Princeton University. It was not unusual then, nor is it today, for trustees to rubber-stamp the decisions of the university administration, but Cleveland, of course, had no intention of being a rubber stamp. He took his responsibilities seriously and worked consistently to fulfill them.

In June 1902, Woodrow Wilson was appointed president of Princeton, the first non-clergyman to hold that position. Cleveland delivered the keynote address at the installation ceremony. It would not be long, however, before fissures opened between the conservative Cleveland and the new university president, whose migration toward liberalism, theological and political, was well under way. In spite of their differences, personal acrimony did not intrude into their relationship. Cleveland regarded his service as a trustee both as rewarding and enjoyable.

At first Cleveland stayed away from political controversy. Before long, though, the old competitive instincts were aroused. He saw too many things going in the wrong direction for him to remain silent. He deplored the Dingley Tariff of 1897, which raised the rates substantially. As president, Cleveland had failed to overcome the powerful interests that supported a high tariff. As a former president, he found, his ability to influence policy was substantially lessened.

While the tariff debate raged, Hawaii returned as a major foreign policy issue. The Hawaiian republic, which had taken power after the overthrow of the monarchy in 1894, requested annexation by the United States. In June 1897, McKinley submitted an annexation treaty to the Senate, but the treaty languished while the Senate's attention focused on the tariff question. In December, the president again called for action. By the middle of the next year, support for American expansion had increased, fueled by concerns that if the United States did not annex the islands, the British, the Germans, or the Japanese would take them over. In June 1898, Congress passed a joint resolution annexing Hawaii, and President McKinley signed it on July 7. Cleveland continued to regard the annexation of Hawaii as a blight on American national honor.

On February 15, 1898, the battleship *Maine* exploded and sank in the harbor of Havana, Cuba. The ship had called there to improve relations with Spanish officials, both civilian and military, to demonstrate American strength and to indicate the United States' interest in an equitable solution to the Cuban civil conflict.

The explosion that sank the ship was probably caused by a fire in a coal bunker, which ignited ammunition in an adjacent magazine,[4] but public opinion quickly blamed the Spanish, whose years of misrule in Cuba deprived them of credibility. The newspaper magnates William Randolph Hearst and Joseph Pulitzer fanned the flames of anti-Spanish sentiment.

Cleveland continued to condemn both the Spanish oppression of Cuba and the violence and savagery of the rebels. He urged the American government to remain neutral. Even after the sinking of the *Maine*, he did not think war was justified, insisting that reasonable efforts to achieve a peaceful solution had not been exhausted. A loyal American, the former president did call for his countrymen to support the government once war was declared on April 25. He predicted that the war would be short because of Spanish weakness but that the acquisition of an overseas empire would be bad for America's national character. Cleveland further predicted that Theodore Roosevelt "will have his share of strut and sensation,"[5] a remarkably prescient if somewhat snide remark. His commitment to the Monroe Doctrine was undiminished, but he adamantly opposed the United States' acquisition of an overseas empire.

Cleveland was correct that the war would be brief and the United States would be victorious. Cuba fell to American arms after a short campaign in which Roosevelt achieved national fame, demonstrating both leadership and heroism in combat. Later in the year, he was elected governor of New York, and the presidency appeared to be within reach. The conquest of Puerto Rico was even easier than that of Cuba, as were the seizures of the Philippines and Guam. The next year, Cuba was independent, although on several occasions in the coming years the United States would intervene militarily to restore order. Cuba leased Guantanamo Bay, on the southeastern coast of the island, to the U.S. as a naval base. The lease is perpetual unless both governments agree to terminate it or the United States abandons the base.

By the 1930s, the U.S. established order in the Philippines, developed self-government, and promised independence, a promise that was not upheld until 1946 due to World War II and Japanese occupation of the islands from 1942 to 1945. Puerto Rico and Guam remain American possessions to his day, having confirmed that status in free elections. The results of 1898 were good for the people of these places. It would appear that Grover Cleveland was not at his best in foreign policy. With the exception of his strong stands in the Samoan and Venezuelan disputes, his preference for non-involvement would have led to less favorable results for the United States and the other parties.

Cleveland's retirement years rolled by, and the new century opened with another spirited presidential election. On November 21, 1899, Vice President Garret Hobart died, presenting the Republican

Party with both opportunity and danger in determining how to fill the void.

Theodore Roosevelt had been elected governor of New York in November 1898, overcoming a faltering start by taking control of his campaign from Republican professionals and finishing strong with a three-week train tour of the state. In town after town, speaking from the rear platform of his private car, he fired up the crowds, never going over ten minutes and rarely repeating himself.[6] He won by a comfortable if not overwhelming margin of almost eighteen thousand votes.

William Allen White, the legendary Kansas newspaperman and later Pulitzer Prize winner, urged Roosevelt to challenge McKinley for the Republican nomination in 1900, but the governor was too politically prudent to heed that call. Roosevelt knew that McKinley would adhere to the two-term tradition and not run again in 1904. The question was, what to do until then? He could run for another two-year term as governor, but he would be out of office in January 1903. In that age of short campaigns, he was concerned about the gap before the 1904 election season. Serving as secretary of war in a second McKinley administration was appealing, but the president was leery of having the independent, dynamic Roosevelt in his cabinet.[7] Senator Henry Cabot Lodge of Massachusetts, a good friend, promoted him for the vice presidential spot, a prospect that simultaneously attracted Roosevelt as a step upwards and repelled him as a post with too little to do.

There were key Republican leaders who considered Roosevelt too independent, and they were horrified by the prospect of his becoming vice president. One of them was Senator Mark Hanna, the chairman of the Republican National Committee, who sputtered, "Don't any of you realize that there's only one life between this madman and the

Presidency?"[8] Drawing an entirely different conclusion about what
to do with Roosevelt was Thomas C. Platt, a former senator who for
years had controlled the Republican Party in New York. Shrewd
enough to back the war hero Roosevelt for governor in 1898, he also
understood that his machine could not control this man. Platt saw the
vice presidential nomination as a way to get rid of him by "kicking
him upstairs." McKinley himself stayed out of the decision, and Roosevelt won the nomination easily.

    William Jennings Bryan still dominated the Democratic field
despite the recovery of the economy, which diminished the appeal of
his inflationary free-silver policy. He commanded an enthusiastic following, while the conservative Cleveland wing of the party had no
effective leader. Bryan shifted the focus of his campaign in 1900 to
foreign policy, attacking McKinley's imperial ambitions and America's
territorial expansion overseas. Bryan hoped that Cleveland Democrats, who shared his anti-imperial views, would overlook their differences with him on monetary policy and that the party would be
reunited. Richard Olney and J. Sterling Morton, who assuredly did
not like Bryan, returned to the Democratic fold for this very reason.
Cleveland himself, however, remained unalterably opposed to Bryan,
whom he regarded as a charlatan. He believed the best course was to
let Bryan lead the Democrats to defeat, clearing the way for more
sound leaders.

    At their national convention in Kansas City, Missouri, the Demo-
crats gave Bryan his second chance at the presidency. His running
mate was Cleveland's former vice president, the silverite Adlai E.
Stevenson. Bryan once again barnstormed the country, delivering an

almost superhuman number of speeches to fervent crowds, while McKinley conducted a conventional "front porch" campaign as he had done before. It was Theodore Roosevelt who took the fight to Bryan, matching and even surpassing him in energy, combativeness, and the ability to stir his audience. The candidates painted the issues in vivid colors. Bryan warned against the malefactors of great wealth and the dangers of imperialism, while Roosevelt warned against quasi-socialism and extolled the expansion of America's beneficent influence around the world.

When the McKinley-Bryan rematch went to the voters on November 6, the Republicans improved on their previous performance. McKinley's popular vote of 7,207,923 was up slightly from the 7,104,779 he received in 1896, while Bryan's tally of 6,358,138 was below the 6,502,925 he received in 1896. No third party played an important role in 1900, though the Prohibition Party did get 208,914 votes. In the Electoral College, the Republican margin of victory was more impressive, 292–155, up from 271–176 in the previous election.

For whom did Cleveland vote? He probably supported neither candidate. During the fall campaign, in a letter to his old friend Wilson Bissell, he expressed both his scorn for Bryan and his hopes for the future:

> I have some idea that the party may before long be purged of Bryanism, and that the rank and file, surprised at their wanderings, and enraged at their false leaders, will be anxious to return to the old faith; and in their desire to reorganize under the old banners will welcome the counsel of those who have never yielded to disastrous heresy.... I cannot believe Bryanism will win.[9]

On March 4, 1901, McKinley began his second, and tragically short, term. On September 6, an anarchist named Leon Czolgosz shot him for the simple reason that he represented government. Infection set in, and the president died early in the morning of September 14. Later that day, Theodore Roosevelt took the oath as the twenty-sixth president.

At a memorial service for McKinley at Princeton University on September 13, Cleveland spoke of him as a man of faith who had displayed kindness, generosity, and patriotism. Cleveland urged the students to follow McKinley's example of character and devotion to duty, and he called upon American universities and colleges to avoid the disintegrative danger of anarchy. He closed with the appeal, "[L]et us determine to meet any call of patriotic duty in any time of our country's danger and need."[10]

Relations between Cleveland and the new president were complex. Roosevelt seemed to have had a higher regard for Cleveland than Cleveland had for him. While acknowledging Roosevelt's ability and courage, Cleveland regarded his quickness of thought and movement and his frequent impetuousness as signs that he was not a person of depth or stability. Here Cleveland, usually an astute judge of people, missed the mark. In addition to being an adventurous man of action and a skilled political leader, Roosevelt had a first-rate mind. Cleveland preferred to consider matters carefully, then act. He matched Roosevelt in courage and strength of mind, but, although very intelligent, his intellect was not as deep and wide-ranging as Roosevelt's.

Roosevelt was perfectly capable of deep antipathy toward certain people—Woodrow Wilson, for example—but more often than not, his cheerful exuberance made him see the good in others. His respect for Cleveland extended back to their run-in over the Manhattan Elevated Railroad bill, when he had come around to the governor's view that it was an unwarranted extension of government power. Roosevelt also supported Cleveland's stand in the 1894 Pullman strike.

Another area of cooperation between these two stalwarts was the 1902 strike against the Pennsylvania anthracite coal fields by the United Mine Workers of America. Roosevelt sympathized with the miners' complaints about long hours, low wages, and dangerous working conditions. But they hurt their cause with the president and the public when they turned to violence and vandalism. As winter approached, the strike threatened the heating fuel supply of America's cities, and Roosevelt came under heavy pressure to resolve the dispute. The miners and the owners eventually agreed to submit to arbitration by a commission appointed by the president. Appreciating Cleveland's abilities and the advantages of having a prominent Democrat on his side, Roosevelt included Cleveland on the Anthracite Coal Strike Commission. The miners won a 10-percent increase in pay and a nine-hour day, while the owners avoided recognizing the United Mine Workers as the miners' agent. Cleveland's service on the commission entailed some personal sacrifice, for he sold his coal mine stock at a loss in order to avoid any hint of having a direct financial stake in the matter.

As the 1904 presidential election approached, there were stirrings of support for another Cleveland candidacy. Bryan's two consecutive losses had diminished his appeal, although his last hurrah was still some years in the future. Cleveland, in his late sixties and in failing health, dashed his admirers' hope and made it clear that he would not run again. Years of intense work, long hours, rich food, and not enough exercise had taken their toll. Cleveland was also convinced that the traditional two-term limit was right. The former president and his wife, moreover, were grieving the devastating loss of their eldest child, twelve-year-old Ruth, who died of diphtheria in January, six months after the birth of Cleveland's last child, Francis. After her burial, Cleveland wrote in his diary, "I had a season of great trouble in keeping out of my mind the idea that Ruth was in the cold, cheerless grave instead of the arms of her Saviour."[11] The Christian faith is clear here, cutting through the personal grief. Four days later, his faith had further penetrated the sadness: "God has come to my help and I am able to adjust my thought to dear Ruth's death with as much comfort as selfish humanity will permit."[12] Soon after Ruth's death, Cleveland sold Gray Gables, partially because of its association with her but also because he feared that the projected Cape Cod Canal would intrude on the peace and privacy of the home on Buzzards Bay.[13]

Cleveland's refusal to run and Bryan's back-to-back defeats left the Democratic Party in a quandary. The men most often mentioned as contenders for the presidential nomination were Richard Olney, William Randolph Hearst, Senator Francis Cockrell of Missouri, Senator George Gray of Delaware, and Chief Justice Alton Parker of the New York Court of Appeals. The national convention opened on July 6 in St. Louis. In his keynote address, Representative John Sharp Williams of Mississippi, the House minority leader, praised Cleveland as a strong, capable leader, lauding him especially for his having been the key figure in repealing the Sherman Silver Purchase Act and re-establishing the gold standard. The delegates' sustained applause—Williams twice had to sit down to wait for it to end—indicated how dramatically the political situation had changed since Bryan's runs of 1896 and 1900.

Cleveland was determined to remain behind the scenes, but he let it be known that Alton Parker would be a good candidate. He would have preferred either Olney or Gray, but he believed that Parker had a better chance of winning.

Shortly before the convention opened, Cleveland wrote to William Vilas:

> I cannot yet rid myself of the idea that Olney or Gray might develop a better candidacy; but neither seems to get a start and Parker has a large concentration of sentiment and pref- erence in his favor; and there will be elements of so malign a character in our Convention that perhaps the Parker solid front could not be broken without danger. [Cleveland was concerned about a Bryan comeback.] There is comfort in the assurance that Parker is a clean, decent man.[14]

Parker, a supporter of the gold standard who had endorsed Bryan in 1896 and 1900, won the nomination overwhelmingly on the first ballot. His running mate was former Senator Henry G. Davis of West Virginia, at eighty-one the oldest man ever to be on a major party's national ticket. The party platform made no mention of monetary policy. Cleveland was gratified that Bryan had been defeated and the Democratic Party returned to a conservative footing. But it was the last time that Cleveland conservatives would ever control the party.

During the general election campaign, Cleveland's gradually declining health limited him to giving only two speeches supporting Parker, although he did write a number of magazine articles advocat- ing his election. A man of honor and ability, Parker was almost in

Theodore Roosevelt's class as an outdoorsman, but he was a dull speaker and lacked the president's charisma. It is unlikely that any Democrat could have defeated Theodore Roosevelt in 1904. He carried thirty-two states to Parker's thirteen and won 56 percent of the popular vote. Eugene Debs, in the second of his five runs on the Socialist ticket, received 3 percent of the vote.

In declining health, Grover Cleveland emerged from retirement to render a final act of public service when he served on a commission to reform the life insurance industry. Thomas Fortune Ryan, the son of a tailor and small hotel manager in Virginia, had struck out on his own at the age of seventeen. Lacking a college education, he went to work for a merchant in Baltimore, then moved on to Wall Street as a brokerage assistant. He rose rapidly and became the youngest man ever to hold a seat on the New York Stock Exchange. Ryan ended up controlling most of New York City's streetcar system, became a dominant force in tobacco, and in 1905 purchased control of the Equitable Life Assurance Society.

The insurance industry, tainted by corruption and imprudent management, had attracted the attention of reformers, including Joseph Pulitzer of the *New York World*, as well as the state of New York, which was launching an investigation. Ryan's own reputation for tough, even unscrupulous, business dealings produced a public outcry when he acquired Equitable. He responded by appointing a commission of three trustees to propose reforms for Equitable and for the industry. He selected an outstanding trio—the inventor and industrialist George Westinghouse, Justice Morgan O'Brien of the New York Appeals Court, and former president Cleveland—men with reputations for integrity and achievement. In accepting the position, Cleveland wrote to Ryan,

> While the hope that I might aid in improving the plight of the Equitable Society has led me to accept the trusteeship you tender, I cannot rid myself of the belief that what has overtaken this company is liable to happen to other insurance companies and fiduciary organizations as long as lax ideas of responsibility in places of trust are tolerated by our people.
>
> The high pressure of speculation, the madness of inordinate business scheming, and the chances taken in new and uncertain enterprises, are constantly present temptations, too often successful in leading managers and directors away from scrupulous loyalty and fidelity to the interests of others confided to their care.
>
> We can better afford to slacken our pace than to abandon our old, simple, American standards of honesty; and we shall be safer if we regain our old habit of looking at the appropriation to personal uses of property and interests held in trust in the same light as other forms of stealing.[15]

Cleveland and his fellow trustees performed impressively, and Ryan supported their proposals. Cleveland's knowledge, organization, and resolution led to his appointment in February of 1907 as head of the Association of Life Insurance Presidents, which was pursuing further reforms in the industry while heading off more government regulation. The reform of the insurance industry exemplified Cleveland's philosophy—integrity and efficiency in a market economy with limited government regulation.

Cleveland's last year as a trustee of Princeton University was marked by conflict with Woodrow Wilson, who sought to reform undergraduate residential and social life by eliminating the "eating clubs," which he considered undemocratic. In June 1907, having received a measure of preliminary approval from the trustees, he arbitrarily implemented the change. The uproar from the university and alumni was immediate. Wilson tried to organize alumni pressure on the trustees but failed, provoking the opposition of the faculty as well. The trustees withdrew their support from Wilson's plan in October 1907, but the university president remained defiant. Cleveland and his fellow trustees had been given a preview of the uncompromising self-righteousness that Wilson would bring to America's foreign policy a decade later.

With the arrival of two more children after he left the White House, the joys of family life continued and deepened for Cleveland during his years in Princeton. He still enjoyed getting away for duck hunting, especially to escape the damp cold of Princeton during late winter and early spring. By the spring of 1908, it was increasingly evident that Cleveland's health was in serious decline. The rugged constitution of earlier years was wearing down, and he suffered from gout, gastroenteritis, failing kidneys, and a weakening heart. In March, Cleveland celebrated his last birthday in Lakewood, New Jersey, where he had gone for the fresh ocean air. When his health failed to improve, he sensed that the end was approaching and asked to be taken home to Westland. Back in Princeton, he and Frances quietly celebrated their twenty-second wedding anniversary on June 2.

While in Lakewood, Cleveland responded to a letter from the editor of the *New York World* asking him what principles and policies might reinvigorate the Democratic Party. In his brief, four-paragraph reply, the former president offered a final reiteration of his deeply held beliefs:

> To be more specific in my reply, I should say that more than ever just at this time the Democratic party should display honest and sincere conservatism, a regard for constitutional limitations and a determination not to be swept from our moorings by temporary clamor or spectacular exploitation.[16]

Needless to say, Cleveland's views did not prevail in his party. The leftward shift that began with Bryan in 1896 would continue with only a few brief lurches back toward the center, such as in 1904, before returning to its long-term change of direction.

During his final weeks, Cleveland's Christian faith sustained him. He was blessed with time to reflect and prepare for his leaving. Beside his bed, he kept a hymnal that his sister Susan sent him which had been used in family devotionals during his youth. Also beside his bed was a copy of the poem "At Last" by John Greenleaf Whittier.[17] A favorite of Cleveland's, the poem had been recited by Whittier's friends as he lay dying in 1892. It opens with a prayer:

When on my day of life the night is falling,
And, in the winds from unsunned spaces blown,

I hear far voices out of darkness calling
My feet to paths unknown,

Thou who hast made my home of life so pleasant,
Leave not its tenant when its walls decay;
O Love Divine, O Helper ever present,
Be Thou my strength and stay![18]

Early in the afternoon of June 23, Cleveland suffered heart failure, and the death watch began. He moved in and out of consciousness throughout the night and died shortly after dawn. His final words before slipping into a coma were "I have tried so hard to do what is right."[19] Whittier's "At Last," which had been so meaningful to him during this time of transition to the next life, concludes,

Some humble door among Thy many mansions,
Some sheltering shade where sin and striving cease,
And flows forever through heaven's green expansions
The river of Thy peace.

There from the music round about me stealing,
I fain would learn the new and holy song,
And find at last, beneath Thy trees of healing,
The life for which I long.

Knowing how deeply Cleveland valued these words gives much insight into who he really was now that he was facing eternity.

That same day, President Roosevelt issued a proclamation in which he said of Cleveland that in the executive positions he held, "he showed signal powers as an administrator coupled with entire devotion to the country's good, and a courage that quailed before no hostility when once he was convinced where his duty lay."[20]

Theodore Roosevelt chose his words with care. This was no proforma statement on the passing of a public figure but rather his sincere assessment of a predecessor with whom he had worked and with whom he had clashed sharply, but, above all, a man he deeply respected for both his character and his ability.

The funeral was small. Attending were the family, close friends, and a contingent of key government officials led by President Roosevelt and Chief Justice Fuller. The service was simple with no eulogy. At its conclusion, Cleveland's friend Dr. Henry Van Dyke, a Presbyterian clergyman, read from William Wordsworth's description of the "Happy Warrior,"

> Who, if he rise to station of command,
> Rises by open means; and there will stand
> On honorable terms, or else retire,
> And in himself possess his own desire;
> Who comprehends his trust, and to the same
> Keeps faithful with a singleness of aim....[21]

The pastor of the family's Presbyterian church officiated at the committal of the body, and the curtain came down on a most impressive life.

EPILOGUE

FRANCES FOLSOM CLEVELAND SURVIVED her husband, who had left her well provided for, by almost forty years, dying on October 29, 1947. A careful guardian of his legacy, she gave access to his papers only to those biographers she trusted, in particular George F. Parker, Cleveland's friend and aide, and Robert McElroy, a professor of history at Princeton. Both men wrote impressive biographies of Cleveland, Parker's published in 1909 and McElroy's in 1923. Frances was also satisfied with Allan Nevins's 1932 two-volume biography. Nevins dealt thoroughly with the Maria Halpin episode, concluding that Cleveland was innocent of any wrong against her and had displayed high character throughout. The first presidential widow to remarry, Frances was wed in 1913 to Thomas J. Preston Jr., a professor of archeology at Wells College, her alma mater. After years in his family kerosene business, Preston had determined upon an academic career, earning his doctorate at Princeton, where he met the Clevelands. After Grover's death, Frances, a member of the board of trustees at Wells, helped Preston secure his position there. After their marriage, he joined the faculty at Princeton. He survived her, dying in 1955.

Esther Cleveland (1893–1980), the only child of a president to be born in the White House, went to England during World War I to do volunteer work. There she met Captain William Bosanquet of the Coldstream Guards, whom she married at Westminster Abbey. They were the parents of the distinguished philosopher Philippa Foot (1920–2010). Esther was widowed in 1966, whereupon she returned to the United States and settled in Tamworth, New Hampshire, where her brother Francis lived.

Marion Cleveland (1895–1977) was born in Buzzards Bay. She attended Columbia University Teachers College, married, and served as community relations director for the Girl Scouts of America. Widowed, she married John Harlan Amen, an attorney who served on the American legal staff at the Nuremberg war crimes trials after World War II.

Richard Folsom Cleveland (1897–1974) was born in Princeton. He interrupted his education to serve as an officer in the United States Marine Corps during World War I. After the war, he earned his undergraduate degree at Princeton in 1919, his master's in 1921, and in 1924 graduated from Harvard Law School. A firmly anti–New Deal Democrat, he was often mentioned as a candidate for public office, including once for vice president; he practiced law in Baltimore.

The youngest child, Francis Grover Cleveland (1903–1995) was born in Buzzards Bay. He graduated from Harvard with a degree in drama, taught English, and was an actor in New York and Boston; he had a cameo role in the original production of *Our Town* by Thornton Wilder. Enjoying only limited success in the large cities, he started a summer stock company, the Barnstormers Theatre, in Tamworth, New

Hampshire, in 1931. Initially a touring company, the Barnstormers settled down after World War II as a resident summer company in Tamworth. Francis continued actively with the company through the last summer of his life, directing a performance of *The Fantasticks* only a few weeks before his death at the age of ninety-two.

All things considered, the Cleveland children turned out well. To be sure, none rose to the level of some other presidential children who became presidents themselves or were generals or governors or senators or famous scholars, but none brought shame on the Cleveland name. Their records were good, their contributions solid and constructive.

AFTERWORD

WHERE DOES GROVER CLEVELAND stand among American presidents? Both conservatives and liberals respect him for his character and his courage. He opposed the war with Spain and the American annexation of Hawaii, positions that would now be characterized as "liberal," yet he defended the gold standard and limited government, positions which liberals decry.

Ranking the presidents is something of a national pastime, and Cleveland generally comes out well, ranging from a high of eighth in the 1948 Schlesinger poll to a low of twenty-ninth in the 2007 Rasmussen poll.

In 1997, the Intercollegiate Studies Institute asked thirty-eight scholars, including myself, representing a range of viewpoints to rank the presidents. Here again, Cleveland was rated high average. (I placed him in the near-great category.) The same year, Walter A. McDougall presented his evaluations in *National Review*. He wrote the following of Cleveland:

Near Great. Perhaps the best candidate for greatness who never got the chance to prove it, he was the only President save FDR to win the popular vote in three successive elections (only to lose the Electoral College on his second race in 1888). His record is sullied by the Panic of 1893, but he championed free trade, broke the Pullman strike to keep the U.S. mail moving, and quashed a sordid bid to annex Hawaii in 1893 even as he hung tough against European imperialists in Venezuela, a man of true principle.[1]

In 2004, James Taranto of the *Wall Street Journal* and Leonard Leo, executive vice president of the Federalist Society, edited *Presidential Leadership: Rating the Best and the Worst of the White House*. They sought a philosophically balanced array of historians, political scientists, legal experts, politicians, and journalists. Cleveland was ranked number twelve, at the top of the above-average category. Suzanne Garment, an attorney, wrote a three-page summary of him, praising him for his virtues of honesty and work ethic, but unnecessarily qualifying and limiting that praise:

> By the end of his second term, the country was facing depression, agricultural discontent, and labor violence. Cleveland's straightforward virtues did not equip him to ride the historic tides. Indeed, in the wake of the upheavals his type of virtue lost much of its political salience.[2]

She concluded her remarks by saying that:

> Today we remember Cleveland mainly for a scandal that cast aspersions on his character. In truth, however, it is his good character that places him in the upper ranks of presidents.

What keeps him from ranking still higher is not any lack of virtues on his part but that he faced an emerging politics to which such virtues did not, for better or worse, seem relevant.[3]

I disagree with these characterizations. Cleveland's virtues and policies are just as pertinent for his own time and ours as they were for the earlier years of the nineteenth century. There is a note of condescension in Garment's praise. A country in which integrity and a commitment to limited government are no longer "salient" will be much the poorer.

There have been considerably harsher evaluations of Cleveland. Richard Shenkman lambastes him in *Presidential Ambition: How the Presidents Gained Power, Kept Power, and Got Things Done*:

He let the trusts run wild. He let the special interests that controlled the Senate sabotage genuine tariff reform. He refused to fight for higher taxes on the rich.[4]

This is unfair. Cleveland opposed higher taxes on the wealthy not because he was a weak-kneed sycophant who "let the trusts run wild." He believed that higher taxes on the productive were not good policy. In opposing schemes for the redistribution of wealth before the disastrous consequences of such policies had been demonstrated in the twentieth century, Cleveland showed his prudence.

Some damn Cleveland with faint praise, acknowledging his virtues but dismissing them as obsolete. Henry F. Graff concludes his biography on this note:

as a result, well before his life came to an end, Cleveland seemed an anachronism—very likely even to himself—but

in his times the people idolized him for his principled fear-
lessness in the role that the contingency of history gave him
to play.[5]

Certainly Cleveland was admired widely and deeply during his life-
time, but calling him an anachronism perhaps tells the reader more
about Graff than about Cleveland.

Cleveland enjoyed little success on tariff reform not because he
was weak, but because those who opposed him held too many seats
in Congress.

Howard Zinn, attacking from the Left, also charges that Cleveland
was controlled by big business:

> When Grover Cleveland, a Democrat, ran for president in
> 1884, the general impression in the country was that he
> opposed the power of monopolies and corporations, and
> that the Republican party, whose candidate was James
> Blaine, stood for the wealthy. But when Cleveland defeated
> Blaine, Jay Gould wired him: "I feel... that the vast busi-
> ness interests of the country will be entirely safe in your
> hands." And he was right.[6]

Many people would regard Gould's statement that business interests
would be safe in Cleveland's hands as high praise since individual
prosperity and national prosperity are tied to business prosperity. But
Zinn hints at either duplicity by Cleveland or ignorance by the electorate. Actually, Gould was making the best of a situation not entirely
to his liking. Gould and Cleveland were not political allies or personal
friends. They had clashed earlier, for example, while Cleveland was
governor of New York, over the fares charged by Gould's elevated
railroad in New York City.

High praise for Cleveland came from the Republican Elihu Root, who served as secretary of war in the McKinley and Roosevelt administrations and as secretary of state under Roosevelt. In his introduction to Robert McElroy's *Grover Cleveland: The Man and the Statesman*, Root wrote,

> He had strong common sense, simplicity and directness without subtlety, instinctive and immovable integrity, perfect courage, a kindly nature with great capacity for friendship and with great capacity also for wrath which made him a dangerous man to trifle with.... His official judgment was never disturbed by any question as to the effect upon his personal fortunes. He had an exceptionally good mind; a still more exceptionally rugged strength of character; altogether a powerful and attractive personality.[7]

Cleveland's reputation is particularly high among libertarian historians. In a study of the American presidency edited by John V. Denson and published by the Ludwig von Mises Institute, Cleveland earns praise for defending and expanding freedom, for supporting sound money, specifically the gold standard, for respecting the states as a check on the federal government, for opposing protective tariffs, and for his advocacy of a strict interpretation of the U.S. Constitution.[8] Ryan S. Walters, also writing from a libertarian perspective, lauds Cleveland's devotion to principle:

> Cleveland also showed remarkable character when it came to the political issues facing the people. Time and again he stood on principle no matter the political consequences. He would rather lose an election than sacrifice his values, he often told his aides.[9]

On these issues, conservatives and libertarians are in general agreement.

Those values were popular with most voters in Cleveland's time. American elections were not yet determined by whose promises of federal largesse were the more extravagant. Government's duties, in Cleveland's view, included the protection of life, liberty, and property, but not the redistribution of wealth. In an 1891 address to the Young Men's Democratic Association of Philadelphia, he warned his audience that "the undeserved distribution of public money debauch[es] its recipients."[10] Redistribution was not only bad economics but, in a deeper sense, harmful to citizens' moral character by discouraging work and saving.

In his classic study *The American Presidency*, Clinton Rossiter ranked Cleveland just below the top rung (in which he placed eight presidents), praising his "persistent display of integrity and independence (symbolized by the 414 vetoes of his first term) [which] brought him very close to greatness in the Presidency."[11]

Perhaps Cleveland's exclusion from the top tier of presidents reflects his lack of personal charisma and the historical accident that he did not lead his country in war or during a time of severe domestic crisis. The Panic of 1893, to be sure, might qualify as a crisis of historic dimensions, and Cleveland's leadership may well have prevented it from reaching the severity of the Great Depression. For historians like Richard E. Welch Jr.,[12] who take for granted that the New Deal was a successful response to the Great Depression, Cleveland suffers by comparison with Franklin Roosevelt. At their most generous, these historians excuse Cleveland's handling of the economic crisis of his second term on the grounds that it would be too much to expect something like the New Deal in the 1890s. Welch's Cleveland was a good man who could not be expected to rise above his own limitations and the prejudices of his time.

Cleveland's greatest achievement was holding the line against the inflationary policies of those who sought quick and easy solutions to the economic crisis of the 1890s, who clung to the illusion that inflating the money supply would increase prosperity for those experiencing difficult times. Cleveland won the battle, but the war continues to this day. New generations, forgetting the lessons of the past, listen to promises of easy prosperity paid for by somebody else. Eventually, though, the country learns its lessons the hard way, changes its ways, and enjoys an economic revival. The dollar was sound in Cleveland's day and for decades afterwards. It can be done again.

Was Grover Cleveland a great president? He was obviously highly intelligent, though his intellectual achievements were not as spectacular as those of Thomas Jefferson, Theodore Roosevelt, or Woodrow Wilson. He was an effective communicator, though no one would place him in the same oratorical class as Abraham Lincoln or credit him with the charisma of Ronald Reagan. In the end we are left with Cleveland's character. He was a strong-willed man who did not flinch at challenges to his principles and policies. Providence or luck, depending on one's beliefs, may have contributed to his extraordinary political ascent, but as mayor, as governor, and as president, he mastered his office with single-minded determination, dedication to duty, and absolute integrity. A man of solid Christian faith, honesty, courage, common sense, and ability, Grover Cleveland deserves to be remembered and hailed as one of the best American presidents.

_____ APPENDIX _____

THE INDEPENDENCE OF THE EXECUTIVE

"**T**HE INDEPENDENCE OF THE Executive" was one of four lectures given that Grover Cleveland delivered at Princeton University during his retirement years. The university published the collected lectures in 1904 as *Presidential Problems*. In these lectures, we see the qualities that made him one of our best chief executives. Anyone who reads "The Independence of the Executive" meets the real Cleveland—a strong, courageous president who understood and exercised the constitutional powers of his office. He relished the opportunity to do right, yet he had the humility to conduct himself strictly within the constitutional limits of presidential authority.

Cleveland discusses one of the chief flaws of the Articles of Confederation—the lack of an effective executive power. The presidency that the Framers established in the Constitution is, in Cleveland's view, "pre-eminently the people's office." It is the only office for which *all* American voters cast their ballots.

Having lost the election of 1888 despite carrying the popular vote nationwide, Cleveland is understandably critical of the method the Framers devised for the election of the president. The occasional victory in the Electoral College of a candidate who has lost the popular vote betrays, in his view, an "unfortunate infirmity" in the Constitution for which a remedy should be devised. But he is curiously silent about what that remedy should be. He allows, characteristically, that "[i]t seems almost ungracious ... to find fault with our present method of electing a President" when one considers the alternatives that the Framers might have adopted. Cleveland exemplifies the prudence and humility when contemplating reform that is the essence of conservatism.

In his discussion of the Duskin-Burnett controversy over the choice of a new U.S. attorney for the Southern District of Alabama, Cleveland explains the details of the case and the constitutional issues involved as Congress attempted to restrict what he regarded as a legitimate presidential power. He won the fight. Satisfied that an injury to the constitutional balance of powers was avoided, he concludes:

> Thus was an unpleasant controversy happily followed by an expurgation of the last pretense of statutory sanction to an encroachment upon constitutional Executive prerogatives, and thus was time-honored interpretation of the Constitution restored to us. The President, freed from the Senate's claim of tutelage, became again the independent agent of the people, representing a coordinate branch of their Government, charged with responsibilities which, under his oath, he ought not to avoid or divide with others, and invested with powers, not to be surrendered, but to be used, under the guidance of patriotic intention and an unclouded conscience.

Here, as on many other occasions, Cleveland showed himself clear-sighted, tough-minded, determined, and patient.

"THE INDEPENDENCE OF THE EXECUTIVE"

I

In dealing with "The Independence of the Executive," I shall refer first of all to the conditions in which the Presidency of the United States had its origin, and shall afterward relate an incident within my own experience involving the preservation and vindication of an independent function of this high office.

When our original thirteen States, actuated by "a decent respect for the opinions of mankind," presented to the world the causes which impelled them to separate from the mother country and to cast off all allegiance to the Crown of England, they gave prominence to the declaration that "the history of the present King of Great Britain is a history of repeated injuries and usurpations, all having in direct object the establishment of an absolute tyranny over these States." This was followed by an indictment containing not less than eighteen counts or accusations, all leveled at the King and the King alone. These were closed or clenched by this asseveration: "A Prince whose character is thus marked by every act which may define a tyrant is unfit to be the ruler of a free people." In this arraignment the English Parliament was barely mentioned, and then only as "others," with whom the King had conspired by "giving his assent to their act of pretended legislation," and thus giving operative force to some of the outrages which had been put upon the colonies.

It is thus apparent that in the indictment presented by the thirteen colonies they charged the King, who in this connection may properly be considered as the Chief Executive of Great Britain, with the crimes and offenses which were their justification for the following solemn and impressive decree:

> We, therefore, the Representatives of the United States of America, in General Congress assembled, appealing to the Supreme Judge of the World for the rectitude of our intentions, do, in the name and by the authority of the good People of these Colonies, solemnly publish and declare that these United Colonies are, and of right ought to be, free and independent States; that they are absolved from all allegiance to the British Crown, and that all political connection between them and the State of Great Britain is, and ought to be, totally dissolved; and that as free and independent States they have full power to levy war, conclude peace, contract alliances, establish commerce, and do all other acts and things which independent States may of right do. And for the support of this Declaration, with a firm reliance on the protection of Divine Providence, we mutually pledge to each other our lives, our fortunes, and our sacred honor.

To this irrevocable predicament had the thirteen States or colonies been brought by their resistance to the oppressive exercise of executive power.

In these circumstances it should not surprise us to find that when, on the footing of the Declaration of Independence, the first scheme of government was adopted for the revolted States, it contained no provision for an executive officer to whom should be intrusted [sic] administrative power and duty. Those who had suffered and rebelled on account of the tyranny of an English King were evidently chary of subjecting themselves to the chance of a repetition of their woes through an abuse of the power that might necessarily devolve upon an American President.

Thus, under the Articles of Confederation, "The United States of America," without an executive head as we understand the term, came to the light; and in its charter of existence it was declared that "the articles of this Confederation shall be inviolably observed by every State, and the Union shall be perpetual."

Let us not harbor too low an opinion of the Confederation. Under its guidance and direction the war of the Revolution was fought to a successful result, and the people of the States which were parties to it became in fact free and independent. But the Articles of Confederation lacked the power to enforce the decree they contained of inviolable observance by every State; and the union, which under their sanction was to be permanent and lasting, early developed symptoms of inevitable decay.

It thus happened that within ten years after the date of the Articles of Confederation their deficiencies had become so manifest that representatives of the people were again assembled in convention to consider the situation and to devise a plan of government that would form "a more perfect union" in place of the crumbling structure which had so lately been proclaimed as perpetual.

The pressing necessity for such action cannot be more forcibly portrayed than was done by Mr. Madison when, in a letter written a short time before the convention, he declared:

> Our situation is becoming every day more and more critical. No money comes into the Federal treasury; no respect is paid to the Federal authority; and people of reflection unanimously agree that the existing Confederacy is tottering to its foundation. Many individuals of weight, particularly in

the Eastern district, are suspected of leaning towards monarchy. Other individuals predict a partition of the States into two or more confederacies.

It was at this time universally conceded that if success was to follow the experiment of popular government among the new States, the creation of an Executive branch invested with power and responsibility would be an absolutely essential factor. Madison, in referring to the prospective work of the convention, said:

> A national executive will also be necessary. I have scarcely ventured to form my own opinion yet, either of the manner in which it ought to be constituted, or of the authorities with which it ought to be clothed.

We know that every plan of government proposed or presented to the convention embodied in some form as a prominent feature the establishment of an effective Executive; and I think it can be safely said that no subject was submitted which proved more perplexing and troublesome. We ought not to consider this as unnatural. Many members of the convention, while obliged to confess that the fears and prejudices that refused executive power to the Confederacy had led to the most unfortunate results, were still confronted with a remnant of those fears and prejudices, and were not yet altogether free from the suspicion that the specter of monarchy might be concealed behind every suggestion of executive force. Others less timid were nevertheless tremendously embarrassed by a lack of definite and clear conviction as to the manner of creating the new office and fixing its limitations. Still another difficulty, which seems to have been all-pervading and chronic in the convention, and which obstinately fastened itself to the discussion of the subject, was the jealousy and suspicion existing between the large and small States. I am afraid, also, that an unwillingness to trust too much to the people had its influence in preventing an easy solution of the executive problem. The first proposal made in the convention that the President should be elected by the people was accompanied by an apologetic statement by the member making the suggestion that he was almost unwilling to declare the mode of selection he preferred, "being apprehensive that it might appear chimerical." Another favored the idea of popular election, but thought it "impracticable"; another was not clear that the people ought to act directly even in the choice of electors, being, as alleged, "too little informed of personal characters in large districts, and liable to deception"; and again, it was declared that "it would be as unnatural to refer the choice of a proper character for Chief Magistrate to the people as it would to refer a trial of colors to a blind man."

A plan was first adopted by the convention which provided for the selection of the President by the Congress, or, as it was then called, by the National Legislature. Various other plans were proposed, but only to be summarily rejected in favor of that which the convention had apparently irrevocably decided upon. There were, however, among the members, some who, notwithstanding the action taken, lost no opportunity to advocate, with energy and sound reasons, the substitution of a mode of electing the President more in keeping with the character of the office and the genius of a popular government. This fortunate persistence resulted in the reopening of the subject and its reference, very late in the sessions of the convention, to a committee who reported in favor of a procedure for the choice of the Executive substantially identical with that now in force; and this was adopted by the convention almost unanimously.

This imperfect review of the incidents that led up to the establishment of the office of President, and its rescue from dangers which surrounded its beginning, if not otherwise useful, ought certainly to suggest congratulatory and grateful reflections. The proposition that the selection of a President should rest entirely with the Congress, which came so near adoption, must, I think, appear to us as something absolutely startling; and we may well be surprised that it was ever favorably considered by the convention.

In the scheme of our national Government the Presidency, is pre-eminently the people's office. Of course, all offices created by the Constitution, and all governmental agencies existing under its sanction, must be recognized, in a sense, as the offices and agencies of the people—considered either as an aggregation constituting the national body politic, or some of its divisions. When, however, I now speak of the Presidency as being preeminently the people's office, I mean that it is especially the office related to the people as individuals, in no general, local, or other combination, but standing on the firm footing of manhood and American citizenship. The Congress may enact laws; but they are inert and vain without executive impulse. The Federal courts adjudicate upon the rights of the citizen when their aid is invoked. But under the constitutional mandate that the President "shall take care that the laws be faithfully executed," every citizen, in the day or in the night, at home or abroad, is constantly within the protection and restraint of the Executive power—none so lowly as to be beneath its scrupulous care, and none so great and powerful as to be beyond its restraining force.

In view of this constant touch and the relationship thus existing between the citizen and the Executive, it would seem that these considerations alone supplied sufficient reason why his selection should rest upon the direct and independent expression of the people's choice. This reason is reinforced by the fact that inasmuch as Senators are elected by the State legislatures, Representatives in Congress by the votes of districts or States, and judges are appointed by the President, it is only in the selection of the President that the body of the American people can by any possibility act together and directly in the equipment of their national Government. Without at least this much of participation in that equipment, we could hardly expect that a ruinous discontent and revolt could be long suppressed among a people who had been promised a popular and representative government.

I do not mean to be understood as conceding that the selection of a President through electors chosen by the people of the several States, according to our present plan, perfectly meets the case as I have stated it. On the contrary, it has always seemed to me that this plan is weakened by an unfortunate infirmity. Though the people in each State are permitted to vote directly for electors, who shall give voice to the popular preference of the State in the choice of President, the voters throughout the nation may be so distributed, and the majorities given for electors in the different States may be such, that a minority of all the voters in the land can determine, and in some cases actually have determined, who the President should be. I believe a way should be devised to prevent such a result.

It seems almost ungracious, however, to find fault with our present method of electing a President when we recall the alternative from which we escaped, through the final action of the convention which framed the Constitution.

It is nevertheless a curious fact that the plan at first adopted, vesting in Congress the presidential election, was utterly inconsistent with the opinion of those most prominent in the convention, as well as of all thoughtful and patriotic Americans who watched for a happy result from its deliberations, that the corner-stone of the new Government should be a distinct division of powers and functions among the Legislative, Executive, and Judicial branches, with the independence of each amply secured. Whatever may have been the real reasons for giving the choice of the President to Congress, I am sure those which were announced in the convention do not satisfy us in this day and generation that such an arrangement would have secured either the separateness or independence of the Executive department. I am glad to believe this to be so palpable as to make it unnecessary for me to suggest other objections, which might subject me to the suspicion of questioning the wisdom or invariably safe motives of Congress in this relation. It is much more agreeable to acknowledge gratefully that a danger was avoided, and a method finally adopted for the selection of the Executive head of the Government which was undoubtedly the best within the reach of the convention.

The Constitution formed by this convention has been justly extolled by informed and liberty-loving men throughout the world. The statesman who, above all his contemporaries of the past century, was best able to pass judgment on its merits formulated an unchallenged verdict when he declared that "the American Constitution is the most wonderful work ever struck off at a given time by the brain and purpose of man."

We dwell with becoming pride upon the intellectual greatness of the men who composed the convention which created this Constitution. They were indeed great; but the happy result of their labor would not have been saved to us and to humanity if to intellectual greatness there had not been added patriotism, patience, and, last but by no means least, forbearing tact. To these traits are we especially indebted for the creation of an Executive department, limited against every possible danger of usurpation or tyranny, but, at the same time, strong and independent within its limitations.

The Constitution declares: "The executive power shall be vested in a President of the United States of America," and this is followed by a recital of the specific and distinctly declared duties with which he is charged, and the powers with which he is invested. The members of the convention were not willing, however, that the executive power which they had vested in the President should be cramped and embarrassed by any implication that a specific statement of certain granted powers and duties excluded all other executive functions; nor were they apparently willing that the claim of such exclusion should have countenance in the strict meaning which might be given to the words "executive power." Therefore we find that the Constitution supplements a recital of the specific powers and duties of the President with this impressive and conclusive additional requirement: "He shall take care that the laws be faithfully executed." This I conceive to be equivalent to a grant of all the power necessary to the performance of his duty in the faithful execution of the laws.

The form of Constitution first proposed to the convention provided that the President elect, before entering upon the duties of his office, should take an oath, simply declaring: "I will faithfully execute the office of President of the United States." To this brief and very general obligation there were added by the convention the following words: "and will to the best of my judgment and power preserve, protect, and defend the Constitution of the United States." Finally, the "Committee on Style," appointed by the convention, apparently to arrange the order of the provisions agreed upon, and to suggest the language in which they would be best expressed, reported in favor of an oath in these terms: "I will faithfully execute the office of President of the United States, and will to the best of my ability preserve, protect, and defend the Constitution of the United States"; and this form was adopted by the convention without discussion, and continues to this day as the form of obligation which binds the conscience of every incumbent of our Chief Magistracy.

It is therefore apparent that as the Constitution, in addition to its specification of especial duties and powers devolving upon the President, provides that "he shall take care that the laws be faithfully executed," and as this was evidently intended as a general devolution of power and imposition of obligation in respect to any condition that might arise relating to the execution of the laws, so it is likewise apparent that the convention was not content to rest the sworn obligation of the President solely upon his covenant to "faithfully execute the office of President of the United States," but added thereto the mandate that he should preserve, protect, and defend the Constitution, to the best of his judgment and power, or, as it was afterward expressed, to the best of his ability. Thus is our President solemnly required not only to exercise every power attached to his office, to the end that the laws may be faithfully executed, and not only to render obedience to the demands of the fundamental law and executive duty, but to exert all his official strength and authority for the preservation, protection, and defense of the Constitution.

I have thus far presented considerations which while they have to do with my topic are only preliminary to its more especial and distinct discussion. In furtherance of this discussion it now becomes necessary to quote from the Constitution the following clause found among its specification of presidential duty and authority:

> And he shall nominate, and by and with the advice of the Senate shall appoint ambassadors, other public ministers and consuls, judges of theSupreme Court, and all other officers of the United States whose appointments are not herein otherwise provided for, and which shall be established by law.

This clause was the subject of a prolonged and thorough debate in Congress which occurred in the year 1789 and during the first session of that body assembled under the new Constitution.

II

The question discussed involved distinctly and solely the independent power of the President under the Constitution to remove an officer appointed by him by and with the advice of the Senate. The discussion arose upon a bill then before the Congress, providing for the organization of the State Department, which contained a provision that the head of the department to be created should be removable from office by the President. This was opposed by a considerable number on the ground that as the Senate cooperated in the appointment, it should also be consulted in the matter of removal; it was urged by others that the power of removal in such cases was already vested in the President by the Constitution, and that the provision was therefore unnecessary; and it was also contended that the question whether the Constitution permitted such removal or not should be left untouched by legislative action, and be determined by the courts.

Those insisting upon retaining in the bill the clause permitting removal by the President alone, claimed that such legislation would remove all doubt on the subject, though they asserted that the absolute investiture of all executive power in the President, reinforced by the constitutional command that he should take care that the laws be faithfully executed, justified their position that the power already existed, especially in the absence of any adverse expression in the Constitution. They also insisted that the removal of subordinate officers was an act so executive in its character, and so intimately related to the faithful execution of the laws, that it was clearly among the President's constitutional prerogatives, and that if it was not sufficiently declared in the Constitution, the omission should be supplied by the legislation proposed.

In support of these positions it was said that the participation of the Senate in the removal of executive officers would be a dangerous step toward breaking down the partitions between the different departments of the Government which had been carefully erected, and were regarded by every statesman of that time as absolutely essential to our national existence; and stress was laid upon the unhappy condition that would arise in case a removal desired by the President should be refused by the Senate, and he thus should be left, still charged with the responsibility of the faithful execution of the laws, while deprived of the loyalty and constancy of his subordinates and assistants, who, if resentful of his efforts for their removal, would lack devotion to his work, and who, having learned to rely upon another branch of the Government for their retention, would be invited to defiant insubordination.

At the time of this discussion the proceedings of the Senate took place behind closed doors, and its debates were not published, but its determinations upon such questions as came before it were made public.

The proceedings of the other branch of the Congress, however, were open, and we are permitted through their publication to follow the very interesting discussion of the question referred to in the House of Representatives.

The membership of that body included a number of those who had been members of the Constitutional Convention, and who, fresh from its deliberations, were necessarily somewhat familiar with its purposes and intent. Mr. Madison was there, who had as much to do as any other man with the inauguration of the convention and its successful conclusion. He was not only especially prominent in its deliberations, but increased his familiarity with its pervading spirit and disposition by keeping a careful record of its proceedings. In speaking of his reasons for keeping this record he says:

> The curiosity I had felt during my researches into the history of the most distinguished confederacies, particularly those of antiquity, and the deficiency I found in the means of satisfying it, more especially in what related to the process, the principles, the reasons and the anticipations which prevailed in the formation of them, determined me to preserve as far as I could an exact account of what might pass in the convention while executing its trust, with the magnitude of which I was duly impressed, as I was by the gratification promised to future curiosity, by an authentic exhibition of the objects, the opinions and the reasonings from which a new system of government was to receive its peculiar structure and organization. Nor was I unaware of the value of such a contribution to the fund of materials for the history of a Constitution on which would be staked the happiness of a people great in its infancy and possibly the cause of liberty throughout the world.

This important debate also gains great significance from the fact that it occurred within two years after the completion of the Constitution, and before political rancor or the temptations of partizan [sic] zeal had intervened to vex our congressional counsels. It must be conceded, I think, that all the accompanying circumstances gave tremendous weight and authority to this first legislative construction of the Constitution in the first session of the first House of Representatives, and that these circumstances fully warranted Mr. Madison's declaration during the debate:

> I feel the importance of the question, and know that our decision will involve the decision of all similar cases. The decision that is at this time made will become the permanent exposition of the Constitution, and on a permanent exposition of the Constitution will depend the genius and character of the whole Government.

The discussion developed the fact that from the first a decided majority were of the opinion that the Executive should have power of independent removal, whether already derived from the Constitution or to be conferred by supplementary legislation. It will be recalled that the debate arose upon the clause in a pending bill providing that the officer therein named should "be removable by the President," and that some of the members of the House, holding that such power of removal was plainly granted to the Constitution, insisted that it would be useless and improper to assume to confer it by legislative enactment. Though a motion to strike from the bill the clause objected to had been negatived by a large majority, it was afterward proposed, in deference to the opinions of those who suggested that the House should go no further than to give a legislative construction to the Constitution in favor of executive removal, that in lieu of the words contained in the bill, indicating a grant of the power, there should be inserted a provision for a new appointment in case of a vacancy occurring in the following manner:

Whenever the said principal officer shall be removed from office by the President of the United States, or in any other case of vacancy.

This was universally acknowledged to be a distinct and unequivocal declaration that, under the Constitution, the right of removal was conferred upon the President; and those supporting that proposition voted in favor of the change, which was adopted by a decisive majority. The bill thus completed was sent to the Senate, where, if there was opposition to it on the ground that it contained a provision in derogation of senatorial right, it did not avail; for the bill was passed by that body, though grudgingly, and, as has been disclosed, only by the vote of the Vice-President, upon an equal division of the Senate. It may not be amiss to mention, as adding significance to the concurrence of the House and the Senate in the meaning and effect of the clause pertaining to removal as embodied in this bill, that during that same session two other bills creating the Treasury Department and the War Department, containing precisely the same provision, were passed by both Houses.

I hope I shall be deemed fully justified in detailing at some length the circumstances that led up to a legislative construction of the Constitution, as authoritative as any surroundings could possibly make it, in favor of the constitutional right of the President to remove Federal officials without the participation or interference of the Senate.

This was in 1789. In 1886, ninety-seven years afterward, this question was again raised in a sharp contention between the Senate and the President. In the meantime, as was quite natural perhaps, partizanship had grown more pronounced and bitter, and it was at that particular time by no means softened by the fact that the party that had become habituated to power by twenty-four years of substantial control of the Government, was obliged, on the 4th of March,

1885, to make way in the executive office for a President elected by
the opposite party. He came into office fully pledged to the letter of
Civil Service reform; and passing beyond the letter of the law on that
subject, he had said:

> There is a class of government positions which are not
> within the letter of the Civil Service statute, but which are
> so disconnected with the policy of an administration, that
> the removal therefrom of present incumbents, in my opin-
> ion, should not be made during the terms for which they
> were appointed, solely on partizan grounds, and for the
> purpose of putting in their places those who are in political
> accord with the appointing power.

The meaning of this statement is, that while, among the officers
not affected by the Civil Service law, there are those whose duties are
so related to the enforcement of the political policy of an administration that they should be in full accord with it, there are others whose
duties are not so related, and who simply perform executive work; and
these, though beyond the protection of Civil Service legislation, should
not be removed merely for the purpose of rewarding the party friends
of the President, by putting them in the positions thus made vacant.
An adherence to this rule, based upon the spirit instead of the letter of
Civil Service reform, I believe established a precedent, which has since
operated to check wholesale removals solely for political reasons.

The declaration which I have quoted was, however, immediately
followed by an important qualification, in these terms:

> But many men holding such positions have forfeited all just
> claim to retention, because they have used their places for
> party purposes, in disregard of their duty to the people; and

because, instead of being decent public servants, they have proved themselves offensive partizans and unscrupulous manipulators of local party management.

These pledges were not made without a full appreciation of the difficulties and perplexities that would follow in their train. It was anticipated that party associates would expect, notwithstanding Executive pledges made in advance, that there would be a speedy and liberal distribution among them of the offices from which they had been inexorably excluded for nearly a quarter of a century. It was plainly seen that many party friends would be disappointed, that personal friends would be alienated, and that the charge of ingratitude, the most distressing and painful of all accusations, would find abundant voice. Nor were the difficulties overlooked that would sometimes accompany a consistent and just attempt to determine the cases in which incumbents in office had forfeited their claim to retention. That such cases were numerous, no one with the slightest claim to sincerity could for a moment deny.

With all these things in full view, and with an alternative of escape in sight through an evasion of pledges, it was stubbornly determined by the new Executive that the practical enforcement of the principle involved was worth all the sacrifices which were anticipated. And while it was not expected that the Senate, which was the only stronghold left to the party politically opposed to the President, would contribute an ugly dispute to a situation already sufficiently troublesome, I am in a position to say that even such a contingency, if early made manifest, would have been contemplated with all possible fortitude.

The Tenure of Office act, it will be remembered, was passed in 1867 for the express purpose of preventing removals from office by President Johnson, between whom and the Congress a quarrel at that time raged, so bitter that it was regarded by sober and thoughtful men as a national affliction, if not a scandal.

An amusing story is told of a legislator who, endeavoring to persuade a friend and colleague to aid him in the passage of a certain measure in which he was personally interested, met the remark that his bill was unconstitutional with the exclamation, "What does the Constitution amount to between friends?" It would be unseemly to suggest that in the heat of strife the majority in Congress had deliberately determined to pass an unconstitutional law, but they evidently had reached the point where they considered that what seemed to them the public interest and safety justified them, whatever the risk might be, in setting aside the congressional construction given to the Constitution seventy-eight years before.

The law passed in 1867 was exceedingly radical, and in effect distinctly purported to confer upon the Senate the power of preventing the removal of officers without the consent of that body. It was provided that during a recess of the Senate an officer might be suspended only in case it was shown by evidence satisfactory to the President, that the incumbent was guilty of misconduct in office or crime, or when for any reason he should become incapable or legally disqualified to perform his duties; and that within twenty days after the beginning of the next session of the Senate, the President should report to that body such suspension, with the evidence and reasons for his action in the case, and the name of the person designated by the President to perform temporarily the duties of the office. Then follows this provision:

> And if the Senate shall concur in such suspension and advise and consent to the removal of such officer, they shall so certify to the President, who may thereupon remove said

officer, and by and with the advice and consent of the Senate appoint another person to such office. But if the Senate shall refuse to concur in such suspension, such officer so suspended shall forthwith resume the functions of his office.

On the 5th of April, 1869, a month and a day after President Johnson was succeeded in the Presidency by General Grant, that part of the act of 1867 above referred to, having answered the purpose for which it was passed, was repealed, and other legislation was enacted in its place. It was provided in the new statute that the President might "in his discretion," during the recess of that body, suspend officials until the end of the next session of the Senate, and designate suitable persons to perform the duties of such suspended officer in the meantime; and that such designated persons should be subject to removal in the discretion of the President by the designation of others. The following, in regard to the effect of such suspension, was inserted in lieu of the provision on that subject in the law of 1867 which I have quoted:

And it shall be the duty of the President within thirty days after the commencement of each session of the Senate, except for any office which in his opinion ought not to be filled, to nominate persons to fill all vacancies in office which existed at the meeting of the Senate, whether temporarily filled or not, and also in the place of all officers suspended; and if the Senate, during such session, shall refuse to advise and consent to an appointment in the place of any suspended officer, then, and not otherwise, the President shall nominate another person as soon as practicable to said session of the Senate for said office.

This was the condition of the so-called tenure of office legislation when a Democratic President was inaugurated and placed in expected coöperation with a Republican majority in the Senate—well drilled, well organized, with partizanship enough at least to insure against indifference to party advantage, and perhaps with here and there a trace of post-election irritation.

Whatever may be said as to the constitutionality of the Tenure of Office laws of 1867 and 1869, certainly the latter statute did not seem, in outside appearance, to be charged with explosive material that endangered Executive prerogative. It grew out of a bill for the absolute and unconditional repeal of the law of 1867 relating to removals and suspensions. This bill originated in the House of Representatives, and passed that body so nearly unanimously that only sixteen votes were recorded against it. In the Senate, however, amendments were proposed, which being rejected by the House, a committee of conference was appointed to adjust, by compromise if possible, the controversy between the two bodies. This resulted in an agreement by the committee upon the provisions of the law of 1869, as a settlement of the difficulty. In the debate in the House of Representatives on the report of the committee, great uncertainty and differences of opinion were developed as to its meaning and effect. Even the House conferees differed in their explanation of it. Members were assured that the proposed modifications of the law of 1867, if adopted, would amount to its complete repeal; and it was also asserted with equal confidence that some of its objectionable limitations upon executive authority would still remain in force. In this state of confusion and doubt the House of Representatives, which a few days before had passed a measure for unconditional repeal, with only sixteen votes against it, adopted the report of the conference committee with sixty-seven votes in the negative.

So far as removals following suspensions are concerned, the language of the law of 1869 certainly seems to justify the understanding that in this particular it virtually repealed the existing statute.

The provision permitting the President to suspend only on certain specified grounds was so changed as to allow him to make such suspensions "in his discretion." The requirements that the President should report to the Senate "the evidence and reasons for his action in the case," and making the advice and consent of the Senate necessary to the removal of a suspended officer, were entirely eliminated; and in lieu of the provision in the law of 1867 that "if the Senate shall refuse to concur in such suspension, such officer so suspended shall forthwith resume the functions of his office," the law of 1869, after requiring the President to send to the Senate nominations to fill the place of officers who had been "in his discretion" suspended, declared "that if the Senate, during such session, shall refuse to advise and consent to an appointment in the place of any suspended officer,"— that is, shall refuse to confirm the person appointed by the President in place of the officer suspended,—not that "such officer so suspended shall resume the functions of his office," but that "then, and not otherwise, the President shall nominate another person as soon as practicable to said session of the Senate for said office."

It seems to me that the gist of the whole matter is contained in a comparison of these two provisions. Under the law of 1867 the incumbent is only conditionally suspended, still having the right to resume his office in case the Senate refuses to concur in the suspension; but under the law of 1869 the Senate had no concern with the suspension of the incumbent, nor with the discretion vested in the President in reference thereto by the express language of the statute; and the suspended incumbent was beyond official resuscitation. Instead of the least intimation that in any event he might "resume the functions of his office," as provided in the law of 1867, it is especially declared that in case the Senate shall refuse to advise and consent to the appointment of the particular person nominated by the President in place of the suspended official, he shall nominate another person to the Senate for such office. Thus the party suspended seems to be eliminated from consideration, the Senate is relegated to its constitutional rights of confirming or rejecting nominations as it sees fit, and the President is reinstated in his undoubted constitutional power of removal through the form of suspension.

In addition to what is apparent from a comparison of these two statutes, it may not be improper to glance at certain phases of executive and senatorial action since the passage of the law of 1869 as bearing upon the theory that, so far as it dealt with suspensions and their effect, if it did not amount to a repeal of the law of 1867, it at least extinguished all its harmful vitality as a limitation of executive prerogative. It has been stated, apparently by authority, that President Grant within seven weeks after his inauguration on the 4th of March, 1869, sent to the Senate six hundred and eighty cases of removals or suspensions, all of which I assume were entirely proper and justifiable. I cannot tell how many of the cases thus submitted to the Senate were suspensions, nor how many of them purported to be removals; nor do I know how many nominations of new officers accompanying them were confirmed. It appears that ninety-seven of them were withdrawn before they were acted upon by the Senate; and inasmuch as the law of 1867 was in force during four of the seven weeks within which these removals and suspensions were submitted, it is barely possible that these withdrawals were made during the four weeks when the law of 1867 was operative, to await a more convenient season under the law of 1869. Attention should be here called, however, to the dissatisfaction of President Grant, early in his incumbency, with the complexion of the situation, even under the repealing and amendatory law of 1869. In his first annual message to the Congress in December, 1869, he complained of that statute as "being inconsistent with a faithful and efficient administration of the Government," and recommended its repeal. Perhaps he was led to apprehend that the Senate would claim under its provisions the power to prevent the President from putting out of office an undesirable official by suspension. This is indicated by the following sentence in his message: "What faith can an Executive put in officials forced upon him, and those, too, whom he has suspended for reason?" Or it may be possible that he did not then appreciate how accommodatingly the law might be construed or enforced when the President and Senate were in political accord. However these things may be, it is important to observe, in considering the light in which the law of 1869 came to be regarded by both the Executive and the Senate, that President Grant did not deem it necessary afterward to renew his recommendation for its repeal, and that at no time since its enactment has its existence been permitted to embarrass executive action prior to the inauguration of a President politically opposed to the majority in the Senate.

The review which I have thus made of the creation of our national Executive office, and of certain events and incidents which interpreted its powers and functions, leads me now to a detailed account of the incident mentioned by me at the beginning as related to the general subject under discussion and in which I was personally concerned. But before proceeding further, I desire to say that any allusion I may have made, or may hereafter make, recognizing the existence of partizanship in certain quarters does not arise from a spirit of complaint or condemnation. I intend no more by such allusions than to explain and illustrate the matters with which I have to deal by surrounding conditions and circumstances. I fully appreciate the fact that partizanship follows party organization, that it is apt to be unduly developed in all parties, and that it often hampers the best aspirations and purposes of public life; but I hope I have reached a condition when I can recall such adverse partizanship as may have entered into past conflicts and perplexities, without misleading irritation or prejudice.

III

Immediately after the change of administration in 1885, the pressure began for the ousting of Republican office-holders and the substitution of Democrats in their places. While I claim to have earned a position which entitles me to resent the accusation that I either openly or covertly favor swift official decapitation for partizan purposes, I have no sympathy with the intolerant people who, without the least appreciation of the meaning of party work and service, superciliously affect to despise all those who apply for office as they would those guilty of a flagrant misdemeanor. It will indeed be a happy day when the ascendancy of party principles, and the attainment of wholesome administration, will be universally regarded as sufficient rewards of individual and legitimate party service. Much has already been accomplished in the direction of closing the door of partizanship as an entrance to public employment; and though this branch of effort in the public interest may well be still further extended, such extension certainly should be supplemented by earnest and persuasive attempts to correct among our people long-cherished notions concerning the ends that should be sought through political activity, and by efforts to uproot pernicious and office-rewarding political methods. I am not sure that any satisfactory progress can be made toward these results, until our good men with unanimity cease regarding politics as necessarily debasing, and by active participation shall displace the selfish and unworthy who, when uninterrupted, control party operations. In the meantime, why should we indiscriminately hate those who seek office? They may not have entirely emancipated themselves from the belief that the offices should pass with party victory; but even if this is charged against them, it can surely be said that in all other respects they are in many instances as honest, as capable, and as intelligent as any of us. There may be reasons and considerations which properly defeat their aspirations, but their applications are not always disgraceful. I have an idea that sometimes the greatest difference between them and those who needlessly abuse them and gloat over their discomfiture, consists in the fact that the office-seekers desire office, and their critics, being more profitably employed, do not. I feel constrained to say this much by way of defending, or at least excusing, many belonging to a numerous contingent of citizens, who, after the 4th of March, 1885, made large drafts upon my time, vitality, and patience; and I feel bound to say that in view of their frequent disappointments, and the difficulty they found in appreciating the validity of the reasons given for refusing their applications, they accepted the situation with as much good nature and contentment as could possibly have been anticipated. It must be remembered that they and their party associates had been banished from Federal office-holding for twenty-four years.

I have no disposition to evade the fact that suspensions of officials holding presidential commissions began promptly and were quite vigorously continued; but I confidently claim that every suspension made was with honest intent and, I believe, in accordance with the requirements of good administration and consistent with prior executive pledges. Some of these officials held by tenures unlimited as to their duration. Among these were certain internal-revenue officers who, it seemed to me, in analogy with others doing similar work but having a limited tenure, ought to consider a like limited period of incumbency their proper term of office; and there were also consular officials and others attached to the foreign service who, I believe it was then generally understood, should be politically in accord with the administration.

By far the greater number of suspensions, however, were made on account of gross and indecent partizan conduct on the part of the incumbents. The preceding presidential campaign, it will be recalled, was exceedingly bitter, and governmental officials then in place were apparently so confident of the continued supremacy of their party that some of them made no pretense of decent behavior. In numerous instances the post-offices were made headquarters for local party committees and organizations and the centers of partizan scheming. Party literature favorable to the postmasters' party, that never passed regularly through the mails, was distributed through the post-offices as an item of party service, and matter of a political character, passing through the mails in the usual course and addressed to patrons belonging to the opposite party, was withheld; disgusting and irritating placards were prominently displayed in many post- offices, and the attention of Democratic inquirers for mail matter was tauntingly directed to them by the postmaster; and in various other ways postmasters and similar officials annoyed and vexed those holding opposite political opinions, who, in common with all having business at public offices, were entitled to considerate and obliging treatment. In some quarters official incumbents neglected public duty to do political work, and especially in Southern States they frequently were not only inordinately active in questionable political work, but sought to do party service by secret and sinister manipulation of colored voters, and by other practices inviting avoidable and dangerous collisions between the white and colored population.

I mention these things in order that what I shall say later may be better understood. I by no means attempt to describe all the wrongdoing which formed the basis of many of the suspensions of officials that followed the inauguration of the new administration. I merely mention some of the accusations which I recall as having been frequently made, by way of illustrating in a general way certain phases of pernicious partizanship that seemed to me to deserve prompt and decisive treatment. Some suspensions, however, were made on proof of downright official malfeasance. Complaints against office-holders based on personal transgression or partizan misconduct were usually made to the Executive and to the heads of departments by means of letters, ordinarily personal and confidential, and also often by means of verbal communications. Whatever papers, letters, or documents were received on the subject, either by the President or by any head of department, were, for convenience of reference, placed together on department files. These complaints were carefully examined; many were cast aside as frivolous or lacking support, while others, deemed of sufficient gravity and adequately established, resulted in the suspension of the accused officials.

Suspensions instead of immediate removals were resorted to, because under the law then existing it appeared to be the only way that during a recess of the Senate an offending official could be ousted from his office, and his successor installed pending his nomination to the Senate at its next session. Though, as we have already seen, the law permitted suspensions by the President "in his discretion," I considered myself restrained by the pledges I had made availing myself of the discretion thus granted without reasons, and felt bound to make suspensions of officials having a definite term to serve, only for adequate cause.

It will be observed further on that no resistance was then made to the laws pertaining to executive removals and suspensions, on the ground of their unconstitutionality; but I have never believed that either the law of 1867 or the law of 1869, when construed as permitting interference with the freedom of the President in making removals, would survive a judicial test of its constitutionality.

Within thirty days after the Senate met in December, 1885, the nominations of the persons who had been designated to succeed officials suspended during the vacation were sent to that body for confirmation, pursuant to existing statutes.

It was charged against me by the leader of the majority in the Senate that these nominations of every kind and description, representing the suspensions made within ten months succeeding the 4th of March, 1885, numbered six hundred and forty-three. I have not verified this statement, but I shall assume that it is correct. Among the officials suspended there were two hundred and seventy-eight postmasters, twenty-eight district attorneys, and twenty-four marshals, and among those who held offices with no specified term there were sixty-one internal-revenue officers and sixty-five consuls and other persons attached to the foreign service.

It was stated on the floor of the Senate, after it had been in session for three months, that of the nominations submitted to that body to fill the places of suspended officials fifteen had been confirmed and two rejected.

Quite early in the session frequent requests in writing began to issue from the different committees of the Senate to which these nominations were referred, directed to the heads of the several departments having supervision of the offices to which the nominations related, asking the reasons for the suspension of officers whose places it was proposed to fill by means of the nominations submitted, and for all papers on file in their departments which showed the reasons for such suspensions. These requests foreshadowed what the senatorial construction of the law of 1869 might be, and indicated that the

Senate, notwithstanding constitutional limitations, and even in the face of the repeal of the statutory provision giving it the right to pass upon suspensions by the President, was still inclined to insist, directly or indirectly, upon that right. These requests, as I have said, emanated from committees of the Senate, and were addressed to the heads of departments. As long as such requests were made by committees I had no opportunity to discuss the questions growing out of such requests with the Senate itself, or to make known directly to that body the position on this subject which I felt bound to assert. Therefore the replies made to committees by the different heads of departments stated that by direction of the President they declined furnishing the reasons and papers so requested, on the ground that the public interest would not be thereby promoted, or on the ground that such reasons and papers related to a purely executive act. Whatever language was used in these replies, they conveyed the information that the President had directed a denial of the requests made, because in his opinion the Senate could have no proper concern with the information sought to be obtained.

It may not be amiss to mention here that while this was the position assumed by the Executive in relation to suspensions, all the information of any description in the possession of the Executive or in any of the departments, which would aid in determining the character and fitness of those nominated in place of suspended officials, was cheerfully and promptly furnished to the Senate or its committees when requested.

In considering the requests made for the transmission of the reasons for suspensions, and the papers relating thereto, I could not avoid the conviction that a compliance with such requests would be to that extent a failure to protect and defend the Constitution, as well as a wrong to the great office I held in trust for the people, and which I was bound to transmit unimpaired to my successors; nor could I be unmindful of a tendency in some quarters to encroach upon executive functions, or of the eagerness with which executive concession would be seized upon as establishing precedent.

The nominations sent to the Senate remained neglected in the committees to which they had been referred; the requests of the committees for reasons and papers touching suspensions were still refused, and it became daily more apparent that a sharp contest was impending. In this condition of affairs it was plainly intimated by members of the majority in the Senate that if all charges against suspended officials were abandoned and their suspensions based entirely upon the ground that the spoils belonged to the victors, confirmations would follow. This, of course, from my standpoint, would have been untruthful and dishonest; but the suggestion indicated that in the minds of some Senators, at least, there was a determination to gain a partizan advantage by discrediting the professions of the President, who, for the time, represented the party they opposed. This manifestly could be thoroughly done by inducing him to turn his back upon the pledges he had made, and to admit, for the sake of peace, that his action arose solely from a desire to put his party friends in place.

Up to this stage of the controversy, not one of the many requests made for the reasons of suspensions or for the papers relating to them had been sent from the Senate itself; nor had any of them been addressed to the President. It may seem not only strange that, in the existing circumstances, the Senate should have so long kept in the background, but more strange that the Executive, constituting a coordinate branch of the Government, and having such exclusive concern in the pending differences, should have been so completely ignored. I cannot think it uncharitable to suggest in explanation that as long as these requests and refusals were confined to Senate committees and heads of departments, a public communication stating the position of the President in the controversy would probably be avoided; and that, as was subsequently made more apparent, there was an intent, in addressing requests to the heads of departments, to lay a foundation for the contention that not only the Senate but its committees had a right to control these heads of departments as against the President in matters relating to executive duty.

On the 17th of July, 1885, during the recess of the Senate, one George M. Duskin was suspended from the office of District Attorney for the Southern District of Alabama, and John D. Burnett was designated as his successor. The latter at once took possession of the office, and entered upon the discharge of its duties; and on the 14th of December, 1885, the Senate having in the meantime convened in regular session, the nomination of Burnett was sent to that body for confirmation. This nomination, pursuant to the rules and customs of the Senate, was referred to its Committee on the Judiciary. On the 26th of December, that committee then having the nomination under consideration, one of its members addressed a communication to the Attorney-General of the United States, requesting him, "on behalf of the Committee on the Judiciary of the Senate and by its direction," to send to such member of the committee all papers and information in the possession of the Department of Justice touching the nomination of Burnett, "also all papers and information touching the suspension and proposed removal from office of George M. Duskin." On the 11th of January, 1886, the Attorney-General responded to this request in these terms:

The Attorney-General states that he sends herewith all papers, etc., touching the nomination referred to; and in reference to the papers touching the suspension of Duskin from office, he has as yet received no direction from the President in relation to their transmission.

At this point it seems to have been decided for the first time that the Senate itself should enter upon the scene as interrogator. It was not determined, however, to invite the President to answer this new interrogator, either for the protection and defense of his high office or in self-vindication. It appears to have been also decided at this time to give another form to the effort the Senate itself was to undertake to secure the "papers and information" which its Committee had been unable to secure. In pursuance of this plan the following resolution was adopted by the Senate in executive session on the 25th of January, 1886:

Resolved, That the Attorney-General of the United States be, and he hereby is, directed to transmit to the Senate copies of all documents and papers that have been filed in the Department of Justice since the 1st day of January, A.D. 1885, in relation to the conduct of the office of District Attorney of the United States for the Southern District of Alabama.

The language of this resolution is more adroit than ingenuous. While appearing reasonable and fair upon its face, and presenting no indication that it in any way related to a case of suspension, it quickly assumes its real complexion when examined in the light of its surroundings. The requests previously made on behalf of Senate committees had ripened into a "demand" by the Senate itself. Herein is found support for the suggestion I have made, that from the beginning there might have been an intent on the part of the Senate to claim that the heads of departments, who are members of the President's Cabinet and his trusted associates and advisers, owed greater obedience to the Senate than to their executive chief in affairs which he and they regarded as exclusively within executive functions. As to the real meaning and purpose of the resolution, a glance at its accompanying conditions and the incidents preceding it makes manifest the insufficiency of its disguise. This resolution was adopted by the Senate in executive session, where the entire senatorial business done is the consideration of treaties and the confirmation of nominations for office. At the time of its adoption Duskin had been suspended for more than six months, his successor had for that length of time been in actual possession of the office, and this successor's nomination was then before the Senate in executive session for confirmation. The demand was for copies of documents and papers in relation to the conduct of the office filed since January 1, 1885, thus covering a period of incumbency almost equally divided between the suspended officer and the person nominated to succeed him. The documents and papers demanded could not have been of any possible use to the Senate in executive session, except as they had a bearing either upon the suspension of the one or the nomination of the other. But as we have already seen, the Attorney-General had previously sent to a committee of the Senate all the papers he had in his custody in any way relating to the nomination and the fitness of the nominee, whether such papers had reference to the conduct of the office or otherwise. Excluding, therefore, such documents and papers embraced in the demand as related to the pending nomination, and which had already been transmitted, it was plain that there was nothing left with the Attorney-General that could be included in the demand of the Senate in its executive session except what had reference to the conduct of the previous incumbent and his suspension. It is important to recall in this connection the fact that this subtle demand of the Senate for papers relating "to the conduct of the office" followed closely upon a failure to obtain "all papers and information" touching said suspension, in response to a plain and blunt request specifying precisely what was desired.

IV

I have referred to these matters because it seems to me they indicate the animus and intent which characterized the first stages of a discussion that involved the rights and functions of the Executive branch of the Government. It was perfectly apparent that the issue was between the President and the Senate, and that the question constituting that issue was whether or not the Executive was invested with the right and power to suspend officials without the interference of the Senate or any accountability to that body for the reasons of his action. It was also manifest if it was desired to deal with this issue directly and fairly, disembarrassed by any finesse for position, it could at any time have been easily done, if only one of the many requests for reasons for suspensions, which were sent by committees of the Senate to heads of departments, had been sent by the Senate itself to the President.

Within three days after the passage by the Senate, in executive session, of the resolution directing the Attorney-General to transmit to that body the documents and papers on file relating to the management and conduct of the office from which Mr. Duskin had been removed, and to which Mr. Burnett had been nominated, the Attorney-General replied thereto as follows:

In response to the said resolution, the President of the United States directs me to say that the papers that were in this department relating to the fitness of John D. Burnett, recently nominated to said office, having already been sent to the Senate Committee on the Judiciary, and the papers and documents which are mentioned in the said resolution, and still remaining in the custody of this department, having exclusive reference to the suspension by the President of George M. Duskin, the late incumbent of the office of District Attorney for the Southern District of Alabama, it is not considered that the public interests will be promoted by a compliance with said resolution and the transmission of the papers and documents therein mentioned to the Senate in executive session.

This response of the Attorney-General was referred to the Senate Committee on the Judiciary. Early in February, 1886, a majority of the committee made a report to the Senate, in which it seems to have been claimed that all papers—whatever may be their personal, private, or confidential character—if placed on file, or, in other words, if deposited in the office of the head of a department, became thereupon official papers, and that the Senate had therefore a right to their transmittal when they had reference to the conduct of a suspended official, and when that body had under advisement the confirmation of his proposed successor. Much stress was laid upon the professions made by the President of his adherence to Civil Service reform methods, and it was broadly hinted that, in the face of six hundred and forty-three suspensions from office, these professions could hardly be sincere. Instances were cited in which papers and information had been demanded and furnished in previous administrations, and these

were claimed to be precedents in favor of the position assumed by the
majority of the committee. Almost at the outset of the report it was
declared:

> The important question, then, is whether it is within the
> constitutional competence of either House of Congress to
> have access to the official papers and documents in the
> various public offices of the United States, created by laws
> enacted by themselves.

In conclusion, the majority recommended the adoption by the Senate
of the following resolutions:

> Resolved, That the Senate hereby expresses its condemna-
> tion of the refusal of the Attorney-General, under whatever
> influence, to send to the Senate copies of papers called for
> by its resolution of the 25th of January and set forth in the
> report of the Committee on the Judiciary, as in violation of
> his official duty and subversive of the fundamental prin-
> ciples of the Govvernment, and of a good administration
> thereof.
>
> Resolved, That it is under these circumstances the duty
> of the Senate to refuse its advice and consent to proposed
> removals of officers, the documents and papers in reference
> to the supposed official or personal misconduct of whom
> are withheld by the Executive or any head of a department
> when deemed necessary by the Senate and called for in
> considering the matter.
>
> Resolved, That the provision of Section 1754 of the
> Revised Statutes, declaring that persons honorably dis-

charged from the military or naval service by reason of disability resulting from wounds or sickness incurred in the line of duty shall be preferred for appointment to civil offices provided they are found to possess the business capacity necessary for the proper discharge of the duties of such offices, ought to be faithfully and fully put in execution, and that to remove or to propose to remove any such soldier whose faithfulness, competency, and character are above reproach, and to give place to another who has not rendered such service, is a violation of the spirit of the law and of the practical gratitude the people and the Government of the United States owe to the defenders of constitutional liberty and the integrity of the Government.

The first of these resolutions contains charges which, if true, should clearly furnish grounds for the impeachment of the Attorney-General—if not the President under whose "influence" he concededly refused to submit the papers demanded by the Senate. A public officer whose acts are "in violation of his official duty and subversive of the fundamental principles of the Government, and of a good administration thereof," can scarcely add anything to his predicament of guilt.

The second resolution has the merit of honesty in confessing that the intent and object of the demand upon the Attorney-General was to secure the demanded papers and documents for the purpose of passing upon the President's reasons for suspension. Beyond this, the declaration it contains, that it was the "duty of the Senate to refuse its advice and consent to proposed removals of officers" when the papers and documents relating to their "supposed official or personal misconduct" were withheld, certainly obliged the Senate, if the resolution should be adopted, and if the good faith of that body in the controversy should be assumed, to reject or ignore all nominations made to succeed suspended officers unless the documents and papers upon which the suspension was based were furnished and the Senate was thus given an opportunity to review and reverse or confirm the President's executive act, resting, by the very terms of existing law, "in his discretion."

The third resolution is grandly phrased, and its sentiment is patriotic, noble, and inspiriting. Inasmuch, however, as the removal of veteran soldiers from office did not seem to assume any considerable prominence in the arraignment of the administration, the object of the resolution is slightly obscure, unless, as was not unusual in those days, the cause of the old soldier was impressed into the service of the controversy for purposes of general utility.

A minority report was subsequently submitted, signed by all the Democratic members of the committee, in which the allegations of the majority report were sharply controverted. It was therein positively asserted that no instance could be found in the practice of the Government whose similarity in its essential features entitled it to citation as an authoritative precedent; and that neither the Constitution nor the existing law afforded any justification for the action of the Senate in the promises.

These two reports, of course, furnished abundant points of controversy. About the time of their submission, moreover, another document was addressed to the Senate, which, whatever else may be said of it, seems to have contributed considerably to the spirit and animation of the discussion that ensued. This was a message from the President, in which his position concerning the matter in dispute was defined. In this communication the complete and absolute responsibility of the President for all suspensions and the fact that the Executive

had been afforded no opportunity to speak for himself was stated in
the following terms:

> Though these suspensions are my executive acts based
> upon considerations addressed to me alone, and for which
> I am wholly responsible, I have had no invitation from the
> Senate to state the position which I have felt constrained
> to assume in relation to the same, or to interpret for myself
> my acts and motives in the premises. In this condition of
> affairs I have forborne addressing the Senate upon the
> subject, lest I might be accused of thrusting myself unbid-
> den upon the attention of that body.

This statement was accompanied by the expression of a hope that
the misapprehension of the Executive position, indicated in the majority report just presented and published, might excuse his then submit-
ting a communication. He commented upon the statement in the
report that "the important question, then, is whether it is within the
constitutional competence of either House of Congress to have access
to the official papers and documents in the various public offices of
the United States, created by laws enacted by themselves," by sug-
gesting that though public officials of the United States might be
created by laws enacted by the two Houses of Congress, this fact did
not necessarily subject their offices to congressional control, but, on
the contrary, that "these instrumentalities were created for the benefit of the people, and to answer the general purposes of government
under the Constitution and the laws; and that they are unencumbered
by any lien in favor of either branch of Congress growing out of their
construction, and unembarrassed by any obligation to the Senate as
the price of their creation." While not conceding that the Senate had

in any case the right to review Executive action in suspending officials, the President disclaimed any intention to withhold official papers and documents when requested; and as to such papers and documents, he expressed his willingness, because they were official, to continue, as he had theretofore done in all cases, to lay them before the Senate without inquiry as to the use to be made of them, and relying upon the Senate for their legitimate utilization. The proposition was expressly denied, however, that papers and documents inherently private or confidential, addressed to the President or a head of department, having reference to an act so entirely executive in its nature as the suspension of an official, and which was by the Constitution as well as by existing law placed within the discretion of the President, were changed in their nature and instantly became official when placed for convenience or for other reasons in the custody of a public department. The contention of the President was thus stated:

> There is no mysterious power of transmutation in departmental custody, nor is there magic in the undefined and sacred solemnity of departmental files. If the presence of these papers in the public office is a stumbling-block in the way of the performance of senatorial duty, it can be easily removed.

The Senate's purposes were characterized in the message as follows:

> The requests and demands which by the score have for nearly three months been presented to the different departments of the Government, whatever may be their form, have but one complexion. They assume the right of

the Senate to sit in judgment upon the exercise of my
exclusive discretion and Executive function, for which I
am solely responsible to the people from whom I have so
lately received the sacred trust of office. My oath to support and defend the Constitution, my duty to the people
who have chosen me to execute the powers of their great
office and not relinquish them, and my duty to the chief
magistracy which I must preserve unimpaired in all its
dignity and vigor, compel me to refuse compliance with
these demands.

This was immediately supplemented by the following concession
of the independent and unlimited power of the Senate in the matter
of confirmation:

> To the end that the service may be improved, the Senate is
> invited to the fullest scrutiny of the persons submitted to
> them for public office, in recognition of the constitutional
> power of that body to advise and consent to their appoint-
> ment. I shall continue, as I have thus far done, to furnish,
> at the request of the confirming body, all the information
> I possess touching the fitness of the nominees placed before
> them for their action, both when they are proposed to fill
> vacancies and to take the place of suspended officials.
> Upon a refusal to confirm, I shall not assume the right to
> ask the reasons for the action of the Senate nor question
> its determination. I cannot think that anything more is
> required to secure worthy incumbents in public office than
> a careful and independent discharge of our respective
> duties within their well-defined limits.

As it was hardly concealed that by no means the least important senatorial purpose in the pending controversy was to discredit the Civil Service reform pledges and professions of the Executive, this issue was thus distinctly invited at the close of the message:

> Every pledge I have made by which I have placed a limitation upon my exercise of executive power has been faithfully redeemed. Of course the pretense is not put forth that no mistakes have been committed; but not a suspension has been made except it appeared to my satisfaction that the public welfare would be promoted thereby. Many applications for suspension have been denied, and an adherence to the rule laid down to govern my action as to such suspensions has caused much irritation and impatience on the part of those who have insisted upon more changes in the offices.
>
> The pledges I have made were made to the people, and to them I am responsible for the manner in which they have been redeemed. I am not responsible to the Senate, and I am unwilling to submit my actions and official conduct to them for judgment.
>
> There are no grounds for an allegation that the fear of being found false to my professions influences me in declining to submit to the demands of the Senate. I have not constantly refused to suspend officials and thus incurred the displeasure of political friends, and yet wilfully broken faith with the people, for the sake of being false to them.
>
> Neither the discontent of party friends nor the allurements, constantly offered, of confirmation of appointees conditioned upon the avowal that suspensions have been

made on party grounds alone, nor the threat proposed in
the resolutions now before the Senate that no confirmation
will be made unless the demands of that body be complied
with, are sufficient to discourage or deter me from following in the way which I am convinced leads to better government for the people.

The temper and disposition of the Senate may be correctly
judged, I think, from the remarks made upon the presentation of
this message by the chairman of the Committee on the Judiciary and
the acknowledged leader of the majority. On a formal motion that
the message be printed and lie upon the table, he moved as an
amendment that it be referred to the committee of which he was
chairman, and said:

> I merely wish to remark, in moving to refer this document
> to the Committee on the Judiciary, that it very vividly
> brought to my mind the communications of King Charles
> I to the Parliament, telling them what, in conducting their
> affairs, they ought to do and ought not to do; and I think
> I am safe in saying that it is the first time in the history of
> the republican United States that any President of the
> United States has undertaken to interfere with the delib-
> erations of either House of Congress on questions pending
> before them, otherwise than by messages on the state of
> the Union which the Constitution commands him to make
> from time to time. This message is devoted simply to a
> question for the Senate itself, in regard to itself, that it has
> under consideration. That is its singularity. I think it will
> strike reflecting people in this country as somewhat

extraordinary—if in this day of reform anything at all can
be thought extraordinary.

King Charles I fared badly at the hands of the Parliament; but it
was most reassuring to know that, after all said and done, the Senate
of the United States was not a bloodthirsty body, and that the chairman of its Committee on the Judiciary was one of the most courteous
and amiable of men—at least when outside of the Senate.

The debate upon the questions presented by the report and resolutions recommended by the majority of the committee, and by the
minority report and the presidential message, occupied almost exclusively the sessions of the Senate for over two weeks. More than
twenty-five Senators participated, and the discussion covered such a
wide range of argument that all considerations relevant to the subject,
and some not clearly related to it, seem to have been presented. At the
close of the debate, the resolution condemning the Attorney-General
for withholding the papers and documents which the Senate had
demanded was passed by thirty-two votes in the affirmative and
twenty-five in the negative; the next resolution, declaring it to be the
duty of the Senate to refuse its advice and consent to proposed removals of officers when papers and documents in reference to their alleged
misconduct were withheld, was adopted by a majority of only a single
vote; and the proclamation contained in the third resolution, setting
forth the obligations of the Government and its people to the veterans
of the civil war, was unanimously approved, except for one dissenting
voice.

The controversy thus closed arose from the professed anxiety of
the majority in the Senate to guard the interests of an official who was
suspended from office in July, 1885, and who was still claimed to be
in a condition of suspension. In point of fact, however, that official's

term of office expired by limitation on the 20th of December, 1885—before the demand for papers and documents relating to his conduct in office was made, before the resolutions and reports of the Committee on the Judiciary were presented, and before the commencement of the long discussion in defense of the right of a suspended incumbent. This situation escaped notice in Executive quarters, because the appointee to succeed the suspended officer having been actually installed and in the discharge of the duties of the position for more than six months, and his nomination having been sent to the Senate very soon after the beginning of its session, the situation or duration of the former incumbent's term was not kept in mind. The expiration of his term was, however, distinctly alleged in the Senate on the second day of the discussion, and by the first speaker in opposition to the majority report. The question of suspension or removal was therefore eliminated from the case and the discussion as related to the person suspended continued as a sort of post-mortem proceeding. Shortly after the resolutions of the committee were passed, the same person who superseded the suspended and defunct officer was again nominated to succeed him by reason of the expiration of his term; and this nomination was confirmed.

At last, after stormy weather, Duskin, the suspended, and Burnett, his successor, were at rest. The earnest contention that beat about their names ceased, and no shout of triumph disturbed the supervening quiet.

V

I have thus attempted, after fourteen years of absolute calm, to recount the prominent details of the strife; and I hope that interest in the subject is still sufficient to justify me in a further brief reference to some features of the dispute and certain incidents that followed it, which may aid to a better appreciation of its true character and motive.

Of the elaborate speeches made in support of the resolutions and the committee's majority report, seven dealt more or less prominently with the President's Civil Service reform professions and his pledges against the removal of officials on purely partizan grounds. It seems to have been assumed that these pledges had been violated. At any rate, without any evidence worthy of the name, charges of such violation ranged all the way from genteel insinuation to savage accusation. Senators who would have stoutly refused to vote for the spoils system broadly intimated or openly declared that if suspensions had been made confessedly on partizan grounds they would have interposed no opposition. The majority seem to have especially admired and applauded the antics of one of their number, who, in intervals of lurid and indiscriminate vituperation, gleefully mingled ridicule for Civil Service reform with praise of the forbidding genius of partizan spoils. In view of these deliverances and as bearing upon their relevancy, as well as indicating their purpose, let me again suggest that the issue involved in the discussion as selected by the majority of the Committee on the Judiciary, and distinctly declared in their report, was whether, as a matter of right, or, as the report expresses it, as within "constitutional competence," either House of Congress should "have access to the official papers and documents in the various public offices of the United States, created by laws enacted by themselves." It will be readily seen that if the question was one of senatorial right, the President's Civil Service reform pledges had no honest or legitimate place in the discussion.

The debate and the adoption of the resolutions reported by the committee caused no surrender of the Executive position. Nevertheless, confirmations of those nominated in place of suspended officers soon began, and I cannot recall any further embarrassment or difficulty on that score. I ought to add, however, that in many cases, at least, these confirmations were accompanied by reports from the committee to which they had been referred, stating that the late incumbent had been suspended for "political reasons," or on account of "offensive partizanship," or for a like reason, differently expressed, and that nothing was alleged against them affecting their personal character. If the terms thus used by the committee in designating causes for suspension mean that the persons suspended were guilty of offensive partizanship or political offenses, as distinguished from personal offenses and moral or official delinquencies, I am satisfied with the statement. And here it occurs to me to suggest that if offenses and moral or official delinquencies, not partizan in their nature, had existed, they would have been subjects for official inspection and report, and such reports, being official documents, would have been submitted to the committee or to the Senate, according to custom, and would have told their own story and excluded committee comment.

It is worth recalling, when referring to committee reports on nomination, that they belong to the executive business of the Senate, and are, therefore, among the secrets of that body. Those I have mentioned, nevertheless, were by special order made public, and published in the proceedings of the Senate in open session. This extraordinary, if not unprecedented, action, following long after the conclusion of the dispute, easily interprets its own intent, and removes all covering from a design to accomplish partizan advantage. The declaration of the resolutions that it was the duty of the Senate "to refuse its advice and consent to the proposed removal of officers" when the papers and documents relating to their supposed misconduct were withheld, was abandoned, and the irrevocable removal of such officers by confirmation of their successors was entered upon, with or without

the much-desired papers and documents, and was supplemented by
the publication of committee reports, from which the secrecy of the
executive session had been removed, to the end that, pursuant to a
fixed determination, an unfavorable senatorial interpretation might
be publicly given to the President's action in making suspensions.

I desire to call attention to one other incident connected with the
occurrences already narrated. On the 14th of December, 1885,—prior
to the first request or demand upon any executive department relating
to suspensions, and of course before any controversy upon the subject
arose,—a bill was introduced in the Senate by one of the most distinguished and able members of the majority in that body, and also a
member of its Committee on the Judiciary, for the total and complete
repeal of the law of 1869, which, it will be remembered, furnished the
basis for the contention we have considered. This repealing bill was
referred to the Senate Committee on the Judiciary, where it slumbered
until the 21st of June, 1886,—nearly three months after the close of
the contention,—when it was returned to the Senate with a favorable
report, the chairman of the committee alone dissenting. When the bill
was presented for discussion, the Senator who introduced it explained
its object as follows:

> This bill repeals what is left of what is called the Tenure of
> Office act, passed under the administration of Andrew
> Jackson, and as a part of the contest with that President. It
> leaves the law as it was from the beginning of the Govern-
> ment until that time, and it repeals the provision which
> authorizes the suspension of civil officers and requires the
> submission of that suspension to the Senate.

On a later day, in discussing the bill, he said, after referring to the
early date of its introduction:

It did not seem to me to be quite becoming to ask the Senate to deal with this general question while the question which arose between the President and the Senate as to the interpretation and administration of the existing law was pending. I thought as a party man that I had hardly the right to interfere with the matter which was under the special charge of my honorable friend from Vermont, by challenging a debate upon the general subject from a different point of view. This question has subsided and is past, and it seems to me now proper to ask the Senate to vote upon the question whether it will return to the ancient policy of the Government, to the rule of public conduct which existed from 1789 until 1867, and which has practically existed, notwithstanding the condition of the statute-book, since the accession to power of General Grant on the 4th of March, 1869.

The personnel of the committee which reported favorably upon this repealing bill had not been changed since all the members of it politically affiliating with the majority in the Senate joined in recommending the accusatory report and resolutions, which when adopted, after sharp and irritating discussion, caused the question between the President and the Senate, in the language of the introducer of the repealing bill, to "subside."

This repealing act passed the Senate on the 17th of December, 1886, by thirty affirmative votes against twenty-two in the negative. A short time afterward it passed in the House of Representatives by a majority of one hundred and five.

Thus was an unpleasant controversy happily followed by an expurgation of the last pretense of statutory sanction to an encroachment upon constitutional Executive prerogatives, and thus was a time-honored interpretation of the Constitution restored to us. The President, freed from the Senate's claim of tutelage, became again the independent agent of the people, representing a coördinate branch of their Government, charged with responsibilities which, under his oath, he ought not to avoid or divide with others, and invested with powers, not to be surrendered, but to be used, under the guidance of patriotic intention and an unclouded conscience.

ACKNOWLEDGMENTS

My wife, Martha, lovingly put up with my frequent preoccupation while researching, thinking, and writing about Cleveland and ably worked on the final polishing. Our daughter, Dana Peringer Moutz, deciphered my handwriting, typed the manuscript, and tracked down most of the illustrations. Editor Thomas Spence at Regnery smoothed out rough places in the text and consistently kept his attitude positive. Finally, I sincerely thank those friends who read the book, made suggestions, and endorsed it.

NOTES

Preface

1. Larry Schweikart and Michael Allen, *A Patriot's History of the United States: From Columbus's Great Discovery to the War on Terror* (New York: Sentinel, 2004), pp. 446–47.

Chapter 1: Beginnings

1. H. Paul Jeffers, *An Honest President: The Life and Presidencies of Grover Cleveland* (New York: Perennial, 2000), p. 336.
2. The city was named after Moses Cleaveland (as the name then was spelled), a distant relative, who surveyed the area and was instrumental in its founding.
3. Jeffers, *An Honest President*, p. 14.
4. Organized as a secret society, its members, when asked about it, routinely answered "I don't know."
5. Jules Witcover, *Party of the People: A History of the Democrats* (New York: Random House, 2003), p. 225.
6. Grover Cleveland, *Addresses, State Papers, and Letters*, ed. Albert Ellery Bergh (New York: The Sun Dial Classics Co., 1909), pp. 28–29.

Chapter 2: Governor

1. As a young man, Cleveland was quite trim, but in his middle years, a heavy work load coupled with heavy eating of rich food combined with too little exercise led to the rather corpulent figure seen in later photographs. He stood 5'11" and now weighed almost 270 pounds. A vigorous man, he gave the impression of being solid rather than flabby according to the description of him by a writer for the *Cleveland Leader*. (Jeffers, *An Honest President*, p. 133.)
2. Alyn Brodsky, *Grover Cleveland: A Study in Character* (New York: St. Martin's Press, 2000), p. 59.
3. Theodore Roosevelt, *An Autobiography, vol. XX of The Works of Theodore Roosevelt* (New York: Charles Scribner's Sons, 1926), p. 76.

Chapter 3: To the White House

1. Henry F. Graff, *Grover Cleveland* (New York: Henry Holt and Company, 2002), p. 52. Part of The American Presidents series, ed. Arthur M. Schlesinger.
2. Jules Witcover, *Party of the People: A History of the Democrats* (New York: Random House, 2003), p. 267.
3. Jeffers, *An Honest President*, p. 104.
4. Ibid., p. 108.
5. Allan Nevins, *Grover Cleveland: A Study in Courage* (New York: Dodd, Mead and Company, 1932), p. 166.
6. Charles Lachman, *A Secret Life: The Sex, Lies, and Scandals of President Grover Cleveland* (New York: Skyhorse Publishing, 2011), pp. 81–82.
7. Brodsky, *Grover Cleveland*, p. 100.
8. Jeffers, *An Honest President*, p. 117.
9. In 1885, about 95 percent of U.S. government employees were Republican.
10. Bissell would be chosen by Cleveland for a cabinet post in his second term.
11. George F. Parker, *Recollections of Grover Cleveland* (New York: The Century Co., 1909), p. 382.
12. Brodsky, *Grover Cleveland: A Study in Character*, p. 15.
13. Parker, *Recollections of Grover Cleveland*, p. 383.

14. Albert Ellery Bergh, ed., *Addresses, State Papers and Letters: Grover Cleveland, 1837–1908* (New York: The Sun Dial Classics, 1909) pp. 134–35.
15. Ibid., p. 130.
16. Parker, *Recollections of Grover Cleveland*, pp. 383–84.
17. Scott Miller, *The President and the Assassin: McKinley, Terror, and Empire at the Dawn of the American Century* (New York: Random House, 2011), pp. 18–20.
18. Clarence B. Carson, *The Growth of America, A Basic History of the United States vol. IV* (Wadley, Alabama: American Textbook Committee, 1987), pp. 14–15.
19. Ibid., pp. 20–21.

Chapter 4: The First Term

1. Nevins, *Grover Cleveland*, p. 195.
2. Brodsky, *Grover Cleveland*, p. 182.
3. Bergh, ed., *Addresses, State Papers, and Letters*, p. 432.
4. Frederick Douglass, *Life and Times of Frederick Douglass* (New York: Collier Books Macmillan Publishing Company, 1962), pp. 534–35.
5. Allan Nevins, ed., *Letters of Grover Cleveland, 1850–1908* (Boston: Houghton Mifflin Company, 1933), p. 62.
6. Nevins, *Grover Cleveland: A Study in Courage*, pp. 228–30.
7. Ibid., pp. 358–59.
8. Cleveland, *Presidential Problems* (New York: The Century Co., 1904), pp. 34–35.
9. Bergh, ed., *Addresses, State Papers, and Letters*, pp. 73–74.
10. A women's college, Wells trained its students in the niceties of social intercourse, such as formal teas, classical music, and art, as well as providing a sound education in the standard liberal arts courses. The typical graduate was an intelligent, poised, and knowledgeable young lady.
11. Brodsky, *Grover Cleveland: A Study in Character*, p. 163.
12. Grover and Frances Cleveland rejected this term, which was first applied to Dolley Madison. He referred to her for formal purposes as "the president's lady." (Brodsky, *Grover Cleveland: A Study in Character*, p. 159.)

13. Probably out of concern that the disparity in their ages would cause him to be accused of excessive domination, Cleveland had "obey" omitted from the vow taken by Frances, making it "love, honor, and keep." (Jeffers, *An Honest President*, p. 179.)

14. Mark Twain, *The Autobiography of Mark Twain, vol. 1* (Berkeley: University of California Press, 2010), p. 386.

15. Ibid.

16. Ibid.

17. The White House grounds still were unfenced.

18. Brodsky, *Grover Cleveland*, p. 165.

19. Robert Higgs, "Why Grover Cleveland Vetoed the Texas Seed Bill," The Independent Institute, July 1, 2003, http://www.independent.org/publications/article.asp?id=1329.

20. So called after the English financier Sir Thomas Gresham (1519–1579), not after Walter Q. Gresham, secretary of the Treasury under Chester Alan Arthur and secretary of state in Cleveland's second term.

21. Historian Robert Allen Rutland asserted that Cleveland's thwarting German ambitions in Samoa cost him in the 1888 election as voters of German background, especially in St. Louis and Milwaukee, switched to Harrison. This may be an interesting point, but the election did not turn on Missouri and Wisconsin. Cleveland carried Missouri in spite of losing that segment of the population and had he won Wisconsin he still would have lost the election. (Robert Allen Rutland, *The Democrats: From Jefferson to Clinton* (Columbia, Missouri: University of Missouri Press, 1995), p. 143.

22. In 1914, following the outbreak of World War I, New Zealand troops seized German Samoa. It is now independent. The eastern part remains American.

23. Ted Morgan, *FDR: A Biography* (New York: Simon and Schuster, 1985), p. 43.

Chapter 5: Defeat and Interregnum

1. Governor David B. Hill of New York ostensibly supported Cleveland but was biding his time in the hope of grabbing the presidential nomination for himself at a future date.

2.   At the time Hendricks died, the president pro tempore of the Senate then was next in the line of succession. In 1886, Congress passed a law putting the cabinet secretaries, beginning with the secretary of state, as presidential successors were there no vice president. In 1947, the system was changed again providing for the sequence to be the speaker of the House, the president pro tempore of the Senate, then the cabinet secretaries. In 1967, the twenty-fifth Amendment to the United States Constitution called for the president to nominate someone to fill a vacancy in the office of vice president, a majority vote by both the House and the Senate would confirm the nomination.

3.   The others were Samuel Tilden in 1876 and Albert Gore in 2000.

4.   Graff, *Grover Cleveland*, p. 96.

5.   William H. Crook, *Memories of the White House* (Boston: Little, Brown, 1911), p. 176.

6.   Graff, *Grover Cleveland*, p. 99.

7.   The firm is now known as Davis, Polk & Wardwell. Stetson was J. P. Morgan's lawyer and Tracy was Morgan's brother-in-law.

8.   The Clevelands' first child, Ruth, was born in 1891, followed by Esther in 1893, Marion in 1895, Richard Folsom in 1897, and Francis Grover in 1903.

9.   This was my home town when I was young and where my family and I enjoyed many summer vacations in later years. Olney's home had a view of Vineyard Sound and of Martha's Vineyard a few miles to the south.

10. R. Hal Williams, *Years of Decision: American Politics in the 1890s* (New York: John Wiley and Sons, 1978), p. 25.

11. Bergh, ed., *Addresses, State Papers and Letters*, p. 280.

12. Ibid., pp. 283–84.

13. Ibid., pp. 262–63.

14. Bergh, ed., *Addresses, State Papers and Letters*, p. 328.

Chapter 6: Back into the Arena

1.   Jules Witcover, *Party of the People*, pp. 273–74.

2.   Brodsky, *Grover Cleveland*, p. 290.

3.   Ibid., p. 291.

4.   Henry Adams, The Education of Henry Adams (New York: The ModernLibrary, 1996), p. 321.

Chapter 7: Second Term
1.   Jeffers, *An Honest President*, p. 256.
2.   Cleveland's second inaugural address was 2,015 words in length; his address four years earlier was 1,651. Benjamin Harrison's inaugural address was twice as long, and William McKinley's first would be almost the same.
3.   Bergh, ed., *Addresses, State Papers and Letters*, p. 349.
4.   Ibid., p. 353.
5.   Jeffers, *An Honest President*, p. 258.
6.   Lawrence W. Reed, *A Lesson from the Past: The Silver Panic of 1893* (New York: The Foundation for Economic Education, Inc., 1993), pp. 57–59.
7.   Albert Ellery Bergh, ed., *Letters and Addresses of Grover Cleveland*, pp. 353–54.
8.   Jeffers, *An Honest President*, p. 274.
9.   Michael Kazin, *A Godly Hero: The Life of William Jennings Bryan* (New York: Alfred A. Knopf, 2006), p. 39.
10.   Reed, *A Lesson from the Past*, p. 71.
11.   James McGurrin, *Bourke Cockran: A Free Lance in American Politics* (New York: Charles Scribner's Sons, 1948), p. 138.
12.   Ibid.
13.   Ron Paul and Lewis Lehrman, *The Case for Gold: A Minority Report of the U.S. Gold Commission* (Washington, D.C.: Cato Institute, 1982), p. 110.
14.   Rutland, *The Republicans: From Lincoln to Bush*, p. 109.
15.   In 1884, the normally Republican Morgan had rejected Blaine and had voted for Cleveland, considering him more honest and his economic positions sounder.
16.   Daniel Lamont was there not because of the cabinet office he held, but because he was a longtime Cleveland supporter and confidant.
17.   Jean Strouse, *Morgan: American Financier* (New York: Random House, 1999), pp. 339–42.
18.   Ibid., p. 344.
19.   Ibid., pp. 348, 350.

20. Nick Salvatore, *Eugene V. Debs: Citizen and Socialist* (Urbana, Illinois: University of Illinois Press, 1982), pp. 119–23.
21. Ibid., pp. 128–29.
22. Samuel Gompers, *Seventy Years of Life and Labor* (New York: E.P. Dutton and Co., Inc., 1957), pp. 222–23.
23. Brodsky, *Grover Cleveland*, p. 344.
24. Witcover, *Party of the People*, p. 275.
25. Ivan Musicant, *Empire by Default: The Spanish-American War and the Dawn of the American Century* (New York: Henry Holt and Company, 1998), p. 28.
26. Gould, *Grand Old Party*, p. 32.
27. Robert P. Green, Jr. in *Historic U.S. Court Cases: An Encyclopedia*, 2nd edition, ed. John W. Johnson (New York: Routledge, 2001), p. 624.
28. "…Nor shall any state deprive any person of life, liberty, or property, without due process of law; nor deny to any person within its jurisdiction the equal protection of the laws."
29. Ibid., p. 627.
30. Ibid.
31. Ibid., p. 628.
32. In these races, most of the "others" were Populists.
33. Jeffers, *An Honest President*, p. 280.
34. Julia Flynn Siler, *Lost Kingdom: Hawaii's Last Queen, the Sugar Kings, and America's First Imperial Adventure* (New York: Atlantic Monthly Press, 2012), p. 5.
35. Ibid., p. 13.
36. Ibid., pp. 62–64, 90.
37. Ibid., pp. 201–5.
38. At that time, Hawaii's population was about 100,000, of whom less than half, about 48,000, were native Hawaiians. About 8,000 were Hawaiian-born of foreign parents, 14,000 European, and 30,000 Chinese and Japanese. James Bradley, *The Imperial Cruise: A Secret History of Empire and War* (New York: Little, Brown and Company, 2009), p. 161.
39. An accomplished musician, she is remembered today as the composer of "Aloha Oe."

40. Cleveland, *Letters of Grover Cleveland*, pp. 491–92.
41. Cleveland, *Letters and Addresses of Grover Cleveland*, p. 378.

42. Ibid., p. 381.
43. Cleveland, *Presidential Problems*, pp. 279–80.
44. Ibid., pp. 280–81.
45. Lewis L. Gould, *Grand Old Party: A History of the Republicans* (New York: Random House, 2003), p. 128.
46. Ivan Musicant, *Empire By Default,* p. 82.
47. Ibid., p. 86.
48. Ibid., p. 88.
49. Cleveland, *Presidential Problems*, pp. 79–80.

Chapter 8: Transition
1. Witcover, *Party of the People*, p. 275.
2. Michael Kazin, *A Godly Hero: The Life of William Jennings Bryan* (New York: Alfred a Knopf, 2006), p. 57.
3. Ibid., pp. 57–58.
4. Kazin, *A Godly Hero*, p. 61.
5. H. Wayne Morgan, *William McKinley and His America* (Syracuse, New York: Syracuse University Press, 1963), p. 240.
6. Robert P. Howard, *Mostly Good and Competent Men, 2nd edition* (Springfield, Illinois: The Institute for Public Affairs, 1988), p. 131.
7. Cleveland, *Letters of Grover Cleveland*, p. 456.
8. Kazin, *A Godly Hero*, p. 64.
9. Democracy as used here meant the Democratic Party, not democracy as a political system.
10. Kazin, *A Godly Hero*, pp. 64–65.
11. Ibid., p. 233.
12. Morgan, *William McKinley and His America*, p. 242.
13. Witcover, *Party of the People*, p. 279.
14. James Ford Rhodes, *The McKinley and Roosevelt Administrations, 1897–1909* (New York: The Macmillan Company, 1922), p. 45. It is interesting to note that Rhodes was Mark Hanna's brother-in-law and was a conservative, Bourbon Democrat.

15. He did have qualms that Chinese immigrants could do so and wanted to limit their further immigration to this country.
16. Williams, *Years of Decision*, p. 117.
17. Morgan, *William McKinley and His America*, pp. 270–71.

Chapter 9: Twilight

1. Westland today is privately owned and is listed with the U.S. National Register of Historic Places.
2. Cleveland, *Presidential Problems,* pp. 12–13.
3. Ibid., p. x.
4. G. J. A. O'Toole, *The Spanish War: An American Epic—1898* (New York: W. W. Norton and Company, 1984), p. 400.
5. Brodsky, *Grover Cleveland*, p. 417.
6. Edmund Morris, *The Rise of Theodore Roosevelt* (New York: Coward, McCann and Geoghan, Inc., 1979), p. 683.
7. As assistant secretary of the navy in 1898, Roosevelt had been brilliantly effective in preparing the fleet for war with Spain, but he had ruffled the feathers of more staid members of the administration who considered him too flamboyant.
8. Ibid., p. 724.
9. Brodsky, *Grover Cleveland*, p. 422.
10. Cleveland, *Addresses, State Papers and Letters*, Bergh, ed., p. 414.
11. Jeffers, *An Honest President*, p. 336.
12. Ibid.
13. After being sold, Gray Gables was opened to the public as a restaurant. Much was preserved as it had been when it was the summer White House, such as marks in the woodwork measuring the growth of the Cleveland children. In 1973, it was destroyed by fire, officially still an unsolved case of arson. Another house, retaining a good amount of the ambiance of the old one, now stands on the site. The neighborhood today is still referred to as Gray Gables.
14. Cleveland, *Letters of Grover Cleveland*, p. 62.
15. Ibid., p. 597.
16. Cleveland, *Addresses, State Papers and Letters*, Bergh, ed., p. 455.
17. Brodsky, *Grover Cleveland*, p. 444.

18. John Greenleaf Whittier, *The Poetical Works of Whittier* (Boston: Houghton Mifflin Company, 1975), p. 463.
19. Graff, *Grover Cleveland*, p. 135.
20. Cleveland, *Addresses, State Papers and Letters*, Bergh, ed., p. 461.
21. William Wordsworth, "Character of the Happy Warrior," *The Poetical Works of William Wordsworth*, Thomas Hutchinson, ed. (London: Oxford University Press, 1960), p. 387.

Afterword

1. Walter A. McDougall, *National Review*, October 27, 1997, p. 34.
2. James Taranto and Leonard Leo, eds., *Presidential Leadership: Rating the Best and the Worst in the White House* (New York: A Wall Street Journal Book, published by Free Press, 2004) p. 112.
3. Ibid., p. 114.
4. Richard Shenkman, *Presidential Ambition: How the Presidents Gained Power, Kept Power, and Got Things Done* (New York: HarperCollins Publishers, 1999), p. 239.
5. Henry F. Graff, *Grover Cleveland* (New York: Times Books, Henry Holt and Company, 2002), p. 138.
6. Howard Zinn, *A People's History of the United States 1492–Present* (New York: HarperCollins, 1995), p. 252.
7. Robert McElroy, *Grover Cleveland: The Man and the Statesman* (New York: Harper and Brothers Publishers, 1923), pp. x–xi.
8. John V. Denson, ed., *Reassessing the Presidency: The Rise of the Executive State and the Decline of Freedom* (Auburn, Alabama: Ludwig von Mises Institute, 2001), pp. xviii, xix.
9. Ryan S. Walters, *The Last Jeffersonian: Grover Cleveland and the Path of Restoring the Republic* (Bloomington, Indiana: West Bow Press, 2012), p. 29.
10. Cleveland, Addresses, *State Papers and Letters*, Bergh, ed., p. 283.
11. Clinton Rossiter, *The American Presidency* (New York: Harcourt, Brace and World, Inc., 1960), p. 106.
12. Richard E. Welch Jr., *The Presidencies of Grover Cleveland* (Lawrence, Kansas: The University Press of Kansas, 1988), p. 127.

BIBLIOGRAPHY

PRIMARY SOURCES

Brands, H. W., ed. *The Selected Letters of Theodore Roosevelt.* New York: Cooper Square Press, 2001.

Cleveland, Grover. *Addresses, State Papers and Letters*, Albert Ellery Bergh, ed. New York: The Sun Dial Classics Co., 1909.

Cleveland, Grover. *Letters of Grover Cleveland*, Allan Nevins, ed. Boston: Houghton Mifflin Company, 1933.

Cleveland, Grover. *Presidential Problems.* New York: The Century, 1904.

Cleveland, Grover. *The Writings and Speeches of Grover Cleveland*, George F. Parker, ed. New York: Cassell Publishing Company, 1892.

Cowles, Anna Roosevelt, ed. *Letters from Theodore Roosevelt to Anna Roosevelt Cowles, 1870–1918.* New York: Charles Scribner's Sons, 1924.

Douglass, Frederick. *The Life and Times of Frederick Douglass.*

New York: Collier Books Macmillan Publishing Company, 1962.

Gompers, Samuel. *Seventy Years of Life and Labor*, revised and edited by Philip Taft and John A. Sessions. New York: E. P. Dutton and Co., Inc., 1957.

Roosevelt, Theodore. *An Autobiography*, vol. XX of *The Works of Theodore Roosevelt*. New York: Charles Scribner's Sons, 1926.

Twain, Mark. *The Autobiography of Mark Twain, vol. 1*. Berkeley, California: University of California Press, 2010.

Whittier, John Greenleaf. *The Poetical Works of Whittier*. Boston: Houghton Mifflin Company, 1975.

Wordsworth, William. *The Poetical Works of William Wordsworth*, Thomas Hutchinson, ed. London: Oxford University Press, 1960.

SECONDARY SOURCES

Anthony, Carl Sferraza. *First Ladies: The Saga of the Presidents' Wives and Their Power 1789–1961*. New York: William Morrow and Company, Inc., 1990.

Boller, Paul F., Jr. *Presidential Campaigns*. New York: Oxford University Press, 1984.

Bradley, James. *The Imperial Cruise: A Secret History of Empire and War*. New York: Little, Brown and Company, 2009.

Brands, H. W. *T. R.: The Last Romantic*. New York: Basic Books, 1997.

Brodsky, Alyn. *Grover Cleveland: A Study in Character*. New York: St. Martin's Press, 2000.

Cadenhead, J. E., Jr. *Theodore Roosevelt: The Paradox of Progressivism*. Woodbury, New York: Barron's Educational Series, Inc., 1974.

Calhoun, Charles W. *Benjamin Harrison*. New York: Times Books, Henry Holt and Company, 2005.

Cashman, Sean Dennis. *America in the Gilded Age: From the Death of Lincoln to the Rise of Theodore Roosevelt*. New York: New York University Press, 1984.

Dalton, Kathleen. *Theodore Roosevelt: A Strenuous Life*. New York: Alfred A. Knopf, 2002.

Denson, John V., ed. *Reassessing the Presidency: The Rise of the Executive State and the Decline of Freedom*. Auburn, Alabama: Ludwig von Mises Institute, 2001.

Gould, Lewis L. *Grand Old Party: A History of the Republicans*. New York: Random House, 2003.

Graff, Henry F. *Grover Cleveland*. New York: Times Books, Henry Holt and Company, 2002.

Green, Robert P., Jr. *Historic U.S. Court Cases: An Encyclopedia*, 2nd ed., John W. Johnson, ed. (New York: Routledge, 2001), p. 624.

Grondahl, Paul. *I Rose Like a Rocket: The Political Education of Theodore Roosevelt*. New York: Free Press, 2004.

Hoffman, Andrew. *Inventing Mark Twain: The Lives of Samuel Langhorne Clemens*. New York: William Morrow and Company, Inc., 1997.

Howard, Robert P. *Mostly Good and Competent Men*, 2nd edition. Springfield, Illinois: The Institute for Public Affairs, 1988.

Huggins, Nathan Irvin. *Slave and Citizen: The Life of Frederick Douglass*. Boston: Little, Brown and Company, 1980.

Jeffers, H. Paul. *An Honest President: The Life and Presidencies of Grover Cleveland*. New York: Harper Collins, 2000.

Kazin, Michael. *A Godly Hero: The Life of William Jennings Bryan*. New York: Alfred A. Knopf, 2006.

Lachman, Charles. *A Secret Life: The Sex, Lies, and Scandals of Grover Cleveland*. New York: Skyhorse Publishing, 2011.

McElroy, Robert. *Grover Cleveland: The Man and the Statesman.* New York: Harper and Brothers Publishers, 1923.

McFeely, William S. *Frederick Douglass.* New York: W. W. Norton and Company, 1991.

McGurrin, James. *Bourke Cockran: A Free Lance in American Politics.* New York: Charles Scribner's Sons, 1948.

Merrill, Horace Samuel. *Bourbon Leader: Grover Cleveland and the Democratic Party.* Boston: Little, Brown and Company, 1957.

Morgan, H. Wayne. *William McKinley and His America.* Syracuse, New York: Syracuse University Press, 1963.

Morris, Edmund. *The Rise of Theodore Roosevelt.* New York: Coward, McCann and Geoghegan, Inc., 1979.

Morris, Edmund. *Theodore Rex.* New York: Random House, 2001.

Musicant, Ivan. *Empire By Default: The Spanish-American War and the Dawn of the American Century.* New York: Henry Holt and Company, 1998.

National Review. October 27, 1997, p. 34.

Nevins, Robert J. *Grover Cleveland: A Study in Courage.* New York: Dodd, Mead and Company, 1932.

Norrell, Robert J. *Up From Slavery: The Life of Booker T. Washington.* Cambridge, Massachusetts: The Belknap press of Harvard University, 2009.

Parker, George F. *Recollections of Grover Cleveland.* New York: The Century Co., 1909.

Reed, Lawrence W. *A Lesson in History: The Silver Panic of 1893.* Irvington-on-Hudson, New York: The Foundation for Economic Education, Inc., 1993.

Rhodes, James Ford. *The McKinely and Roosevelt Administrations, 1897–1909.* (New York: The Macmillan Company, 1922), p. 45.

Roberts, Andrew. "The Whale Against the Wolf" in Robert Cowley, ed. *What If? Eminent Historians Imagine What Might Have Been.* New York: G. P. Putnam's Sons, 2003.

Salvatore, Nick. *Eugene V. Debs: Citizen and Socialist.* Urbana, Illinois: University of Illinois Press, 1982.

Schweikart, Larry, and Michael Allen. *A Patriot's History of the United States: From Columbus's Great Discovery to the War on Terror.* New York: Sentinel, 2004.

Shenkman, Richard. *Presidential Ambition: How the Presidents Gained Power, Kept Power, and Got Things Done.* New York: HarperCollins Publishers, 1999.

Siler, Julia Flynn. *Lost Kingdom: Hawaii's Lost Queen, the Sugar Kings, and America's First Imperial Adventure.* New York: Atlantic Monthly Press, 2012.

Smith, Page. *The Rise of Industrial America,* vol. 6 of *A Peoples' History of the Post-Reconstruction Era.* New York: McGraw-Hill Book Company, 1984.

Strouse, Jean. *Morgan: American Financier.* New York: Random House, 1999

Traxel, David. *Crusader Nation: United States in Peace and the Great War, 1898–1920.* New York: Alfred A. Knopf, 2006.

Truman, Margaret. *First Ladies.* New York: Random House, 1994.

Tugwell, Rexford G. *Grover Cleveland.* New York: The Macmillan Company, 1968.

Walters, Ryan S. *The Last Jeffersonian: Grover Cleveland and the Path to Restoring the Republic.* Bloomington, Indiana: WestBow Press, 2012.

Wead, Doug. *All the Presidents' Children: Triumph and Tragedy in the Lives of America's First Families.* New York: Atria Books, 2003.

Welch, Richard E., Jr. *The Presidencies of Grover Cleveland.* Lawrence, Kansas: The University Press of Kansas, 1988.

Whalen, Thomas J. *A Higher Purpose: Profiles in Presidential Courage*. Chicago: Ivan R. Dee, 2007.

Williams, R. Hal. *Years of Decision: American Politics in the 1890s*. New York: John Wiley and Sons, 1978.

Witcover, Jules. *Party of the People: A History of the Democrats*. New York: Random House, 2003.

Zinn, Howard. *A People's History of the United States 1492–Present*. New York: HarperCollins, 1995.

INDEX